"We need to talk"

Tough Conversations
with Your
Employee

From Performance Reviews to Terminations
Tackle Any Topic with Sensitivity and Smarts.

LYNNE EISAGUIRRE

Avon, Massachusetts

Published by
Adams Media, an F+W Media Company
57 Littlefield Street, Avon, MA 02322. U.S.A.
www.adamsmedia.com

ISBN 10: 1-59869-880-X
ISBN 13: 978-1-59869-880-0

Printed in the United States of America.

J I H G F E D C B A

Library of Congress Cataloging-in-Publication Data
is available from the publisher.

This publication is designed to provide accurate and authoritative
information with regard to the subject matter covered. It is sold with
the understanding that the publisher is not engaged in rendering legal,
accounting, or other professional advice. If legal advice or other expert
assistance is required, the services of a competent professional person
should be sought.
> —From a *Declaration of Principles* jointly adopted
> by a Committee of the American Bar Association
> and a Committee of Publishers and Associations

Many of the designations used by manufacturers and sellers to distin-
guish their product are claimed as trademarks. Where those designations appear in this book and Adams Media was aware of a trademark
claim, the designations have been printed with initial capital letters.

This book is available at quantity discounts for bulk purchases.
For information, please call 1-800-289-0963.

Contents

Acknowledgments

As I finish this, my sixth book, I realize that teams, not just authors, produce books. I am grateful for my own dream team. I'm indebted to my agent, Michael Snell, who came to me with the proposal for this book. Chelsea King at Adams Media created the original concept, and helped me shape and refocus the content, while remaining cheerful and optimistic—everything a writer wants in an editor. Brendan O'Neill also brought his expert editorial pen to the process.

On the home front, my hard-working and upbeat assistant, Shannon Duran, typed and proofed endless versions of this book without complaint. O. C. O'Connell offered last-minute editing. I'm thankful to many clients who trusted me with their personal stories. Their names and identities have been changed in many situations to protect the innocent.

Friends Bill Cahal, Susan Hazaleus, and Val Moses helped shore up my attitude. My fellow "villagers," residents of my co-housing community in Golden, Colorado, offered in-the-trenches training on the realities of creating productive conversations and dialogues instead of debates.

My parents, Joe and Wilma Eisaguirre, and siblings, Kim Jones and Lew Eisaguirre, provided moral support and their usual unflagging belief in my abilities—besides teaching me much of what I know about difficult conversations! (That's a joke, guys!)

On the home front, Nancy Fox helped care for my children with devoted attention so that I would have the time and energy to work. John Evans provided moral support as well as extra child care. And of course my kids, Elizabeth and Nicholas, worked cheerfully on their own books so that I would have the time to write mine. I love you more than any writer's words can ever express.

Introduction

If you're like most managers, you spend your days responding to many e-mails and voice mails, and towering stacks of correspondence.

You may also have your own responsibilities as an individual contributor. In the midst of this chaos, you have a problem employee that you know you need to talk to about a performance problem, a leave request, a discrimination complaint, or another dicey issue. But this task goes to the bottom of the pile for one very big reason: You have absolutely, positively, no idea what you're going to say!

Sound familiar? Managers go through this every day in offices, factories, schools, and stores around the country. They know they need to talk to someone about something challenging but have no idea how to begin—much less end—these difficult conversations. Longing for a dialogue coach or a scriptwriter in the sky so they could just crib notes, they delay until things escalate beyond repair and then sally forth and create chaos. Why doesn't someone save them?

Now someone has. With *"We Need to Talk": Tough Conversations with Your Employee*, you have at your fingertips a detailed and easy-to-read guide about what to say and what not to say in high-stakes situations. Complete with real-world examples, general information, and tips, each chapter provides a script so that you can't go wrong in your next difficult dialogue.

This book is not an academic tome but a practical guide through such topics as leave requests, discipline, performance management, and terminations. Using vivid examples, expert commentary, and useful scripts, this book will give you the words and tools you need to navigate workplace conundrums with grace and success. "*We Need to Talk*": *Tough Conversations with Your Employee*, presents a step-by-step guide through the most common difficult conversations that bosses need to have with employees. This book isn't an oversized textbook, but a practical "how-to" guide that dives straight to the issues, offering real answers that work in those difficult workplace dialogue dilemmas. Topics such as leave requests, disability discussions, complaints, performance issues, raises, promotion requests, and performance reviews are all presented in this pragmatic and proven approach.

Using vivid examples, expert commentary, and useful scripts, this book will give you the words and tools you need to navigate workplace conundrums with grace and success.

A Disclaimer, Since I'm an Attorney

If you have a human resources department or director in your organization, it's always a good idea to try to seek advice or counsel there. If used before you visit HR, this book will give you a general idea of what to say—and perhaps more important, what not to say—but it can't give you the specifics of your organization's policies and culture, which can be critical. Don't overlook these important nuances. Your HR department wants you to have a successful relationship with your employee, and you can benefit from spending time with an HR professional before you talk with your employee.

Of course, there remain certain circumstances in which you'll need to consult an attorney, regardless of the tools in this book. This book is not meant to be legal advice: that can only be gained through a consultation with your own attorney and by developing an attorney-client relationship. The information here is offered for educational purposes only. What this book may do, however, is help you decide when you need to consult an attorney and when you can go it alone. *This book is not a substitute for competent legal advice.*

Employee Communication Don'ts	Employee Communication Dos
Avoid conflict.	Embrace conflict as a call to change.
Rely on outdated skills or instinct.	Learn conflict and communication skills.

Chapter 1

How to Get Your Employees to Do What You Say

DEBRA SANDERS PULLED on her high-heeled shoes and stood up. Maybe the extra three inches would give her the height her five-foot frame needed. She'd only been a manager six months and already she felt as if she'd failed. No one seemed to respect her authority. Her team swarmed around the office like an unruly pack of teenagers, throwing paper airplanes, surfing the Net, going out for coffee, quarreling, and gossiping. Debra needed to have a talk with them, that's for sure. The problem was she had no idea what to say!

Managers Have Rights and Responsibilities

Let's get one thing perfectly clear. You have a right to manage. Many managers, in today's environment, seem confused about this. They wimp out and don't fulfill their responsibilities to the company and to their employees.

Employees are not children, even though they may sometimes act that way. They have to do what you say, assuming that what you're asking them to do is legal, ethical, and consistent with your organization's policies; otherwise, you can terminate them.

Before we talk about more specific conversations, let's review the basics.

With all the employment litigation and general employee grousing these days, it can be easy for a manager or supervisor to feel as if he or she is under siege. Employees complain at the first opportunity about workload, coworkers, and the "lies" they believe upper management is telling them.

In modern workplaces, where just answering e-mail can take up half of all your productive hours, it's easy to lose sight of the big picture: *You are the boss!* If you're a manager or supervisor, you do have rights. These rights can and should help you manage difficult employees. Your rights are limited to three, but they're big ones. You have the right to:

1. Require compliance with your directives;
2. Change standards and assignments; and
3. Require excellence.

Let's take those one at a time.

Require Compliance with Your Directives

As long as what you're asking your employees to do isn't illegal, immoral, or unethical, they must do what you ask. Failure to do so is *insubordination*. This legal term doesn't just refer to military service; it's a hallmark of employment law. Employees must do what you ask, and if they don't, they can be fired or disciplined. They may think that what you're asking them to do is silly or stupid and they may be right. They may think that someone made a mistake making you the boss but regardless of whatever else you are, you are always the boss. You can ultimately terminate them if they refuse to recognize this painful truth—as long as you have followed the proper steps and have the proper documentation. (More about that later.)

Instead of asserting this right, many managers wimp out! Why? Many reasons, such as

- Unreasonable lawsuit paranoia;
- Conflict avoidance;
- Fear of losing a friend/colleague;
- Ignorance of their rights; and
- Feeling too busy.

Regardless of what you think your reasons are for avoiding the difficult conversations that you need to have, you still must have them. Many managers do fear conflict and want to avoid it. One of the best things you can do to improve your management skills is to reframe your attitude about conflict. You need to realize that conflict is not something to be avoided but a part of life and something that can actually lead to higher performance and more creativity in the workplace. That's because conflict provides the creative energy that leads to innovation and productivity. You need to hear everyone out and come up with better ideas than you might have collected as individuals.

In order to make this leap, you need to have good conflict skills. You can acquire conflict skills, just as you would any other new skill, such as learning a new computer program or salsa dancing steps.

The key is to step back from the emotion of the moment and use the rational part of your brain to activate the skills you need. It's easy to become emotional about employee matters. Most of us spend as much time—or more—at work than we do with our families. Employees can end up pushing our buttons just as our family members do. So the key is to take a deep breath, calm down the "fight or flight" response that you have in response to stress, and follow a few simple steps that you'll acquire in other parts of this book.

If You're Worried about Lawsuits

Many managers have an unreasonable lawsuit paranoia and will avoid saying anything for fear that it will be used against them. That will not serve you in the long run. Although employment litigation is booming, if you follow the rules of this book, as well as your employer's policies, your chance of being sued will diminish substantially. As you will learn, most employment law turns on being *fair*, a value with which most people would agree. If you're confused about a specific employee interaction, you can always fall back to that position to ask yourself whether the action you're going to take is fair to the employees involved.

Employees and Friends

Another reason that many managers avoid having difficult conversations with their employees is because they may be friends with them and are afraid of losing that friendship. While it's understandable that you may want to be friendly with your employees, you should be cautious about relying on them as friends. Having employees as friends presents an inherent conflict of interest when you need to tackle a tough conversation. You have an obligation to keep employee matters confidential and to maintain objectivity. If you're close friends with some of your employees, they may press you about conversations that you're having with others, and confidentiality may be more difficult to maintain. In addition, if you're friends with an employee, it's only natural that you will have more trouble being objective about his or her performance.

> "We need to talk"
>
> As hard as it may be to create distance in a friendship, you'd be well advised to do so. Otherwise, you'll be trying to serve the proverbial two masters.

Finding the Time to Have a Conversation

One of the biggest reasons for delaying needed conversations is the sheer weight of management responsibilities these days. One recent study showed that employees of *Fortune* 1,000 companies send and receive an average of 178 messages every day by telephone, fax, e-mail, pager, and voice mail. Managers used to be overwhelmed with stacks of paper. Now, electronic communication multiplies like rabbits. Just staying organized is a full-time job.

Ten years ago, a book called *Data Smog* warned that information is like pollution: You must control the flow, or you'll die from suffocation. British psychologist David Lewis coined the term *information fatigue syndrome* and predicted the toll that data deluge now takes on most managers' performance and health.

"Having too much information can be as dangerous as having too little," Lewis wrote. "Among other problems it can lead to paralysis of analysis, making it far harder to find the right solutions or make the best decisions."

Information overload from cell phones, electronic message boards, e-mails, and TV wreaks havoc with our health.

According to the March 2008 issue of *Consumer Reports on Health*, researchers at Johns Hopkins University studied stress in a group of 1,000 people from ages fifty to seventy and "found that the most stressed subjects, as indicated by high salivary levels of the stress hormone cortisol, performed worse on nearly every measure of cognitive function, including language, processing speed, hand-eye coordination, verbal memory and the ability to plan and carry out tasks."

Managers under attack from execs above and employees below have a hard time escaping this data deluge and finding a way to calm down enough to move into a challenging conversation.

Real dialogue with an employee takes time, energy, and a low enough stress level to manage your own emotions. If you find you're delaying a conversation that you know you need to have, stress and overload may be the reason.

The Employee's Side

In addition to rights, employees also have responsibilities. They must:

- Show up for work on time;
- Perform their jobs with reasonable care;
- Work well with others; and
- Give their undivided loyalty to the company.

Showing up on time, for example, should be a basic requirement in most environments, unless you have a totally telecommuting staff.

Even if you have flextime or core hours, you can require your employees to be there at certain times. With a telecommuting environment, you can require employees to log in to your computer network or be available for certain telephone check-ins.

You may want to give star performers some latitude and not require the same frequent check-ins that you insist upon for other employees, but you do need to be consistent across job classifications, and you need to micro-manage people who are having performance problems.

> *"We need to talk"*
>
> Micro-management gets a bad rap, but it's necessary for employees who are having performance problems and for new employees.

Working Well with Others

Employees also have a responsibility to work well with others. If you have employees quarrelling like four-year-olds in a sandbox, you can and should direct *them* to learn how to cooperate. As a manager, you can tell all your difficult employees that they must work well with others. If they don't know how to do so, you can send them to class, buy them books or CDs, or bring in an expert facilitator, but the bottom line is that cooperation is a mandatory skill in today's workplace.

With warring employees, you sometimes just have to lock them in a room until they figure it out. (Assuming that they don't have a propensity for violence!) If you're going to try this, you should send in a facilitator or other conflict management expert. What you should *not* do is make cooperation and civil behavior your responsibility when it's clearly theirs.

Employees may quibble that they don't have to like the people that they work with or that their coworkers are idiots or incompetent, but they still have to learn how to work well with them—no matter what they think of their abilities. If they whine that "working well with others" is not in their job descriptions, you can simply inform them that "now it is."

Company Loyalty

Full-time employees also have an obligation to give their undivided loyalty to the company. What that means is that they can't have outside relationships that create a conflict of interest or a second job that makes them so tired they can't perform for you. If, for example, you find that an employee has started selling items on eBay and that takes up so much of her time that she can't function at work, you can focus on her nonperformance at work, no matter how good she might feel her excuse might be. If you find that John has started a company that directly competes with your line of business and has stolen your trade secrets in order to do so, you can terminate him.

"We need to talk"

If you find out about these kinds of divided loyalties, you can discipline or terminate employees who won't change their allegiances.

If you have employees who are not meeting these basic employee responsibilities, they're not just difficult—they are failing to meet performance standards. You have a right to coach, counsel, and warn them. If they don't shape up, you can put them on a performance improvement plan and ultimately terminate them if necessary.

Change Standards and Assignments

Employees frequently lament and balk when you try to change standards or assignments and say things like, "My previous manager didn't make me do that." You may be tempted to reply, "Do I look like your previous manager?" and perhaps you should, but the bottom line is that you can have your own standards, as long as they're legal, ethical, and consistent with your organization's policies.

For example, Sarah came to me when she acquired a new team that had very little discipline. Their last manager had been lax. Thus, projects were turned in late, workers pointed fingers at each other, people worked odd hours or not at all, and gossip ran rampant. "How can I convince them to change when they've had such bad management?" she cried.

I advised Sarah that she could and should start fresh. Employees won't like the change and it won't be easy, but you need to make it clear that things will be different going forward and you must lay out specific expectations.

One easy way to do this, if you're a new supervisor or you gain new employees who appear to be difficult, is to have one-on-ones with each employee in which you set forth your goals, standards, and objectives. Then send them away and have them e-mail back to you their understanding of what you said. Trust me, you'll be depressed. You'll decide that human communication is hopeless, because what comes back will be different from what you think you said. You can, however, use this as the opportunity to correct their misconceptions. It also demonstrates that you bent over backward in trying to communicate with them and be fair.

Even after they've been working for you for a while, you should continue to have these one-on-ones with them. Again, ask them to e-mail back their understanding of what you said. Again, you'll despair, and think they're speaking a different language. If you persevere in correcting these miscommunications, you'll have an excellent documentation trail (for which they did most of the work). This also makes writing performance reviews much easier.

Require Excellence

Employees cannot get away with sloppy, substandard work. You have a right to insist on high performance standards, and you should. As long as you've clearly explained what behavior (not attitude, or other vague terms) you need from employees, they must conform to your standards.

"We need to talk"

If you're a manager who inherits a new group, you can and should sit the group down and "clear the decks." Inform them that you're going to be starting fresh with them and that you expect them to do the same, even if you do things differently than their previous manager. You then can have the one-on-ones with them as described above, but you will have set the stage.

Once when I was explaining this to a class of managers, an HR director informed me that they couldn't require everyone to be excellent, since they had to do performance reviews on a curve and a certain number of people had to be rated as underperforming. Well that's a backwards (although somewhat popular) way to run a company. The reality is that you *can* require everyone to be excellent—and why wouldn't you want them to be?

Managers' Responsibilities

Likewise, managers have the responsibility to

- Give employees honest and specific performance feedback;
- Set expectations and standards;
- Follow the law and corporate policies;
- Be honest and fair;
- Document events; and
- Be open to employee feedback.

The first five standards are based on the law; the last is not, but it is very good management and will save you a world of hurt.

Documenting and Feedback

Documenting events and giving performance feedback are difficult, but you must learn these skills.

When you're documenting or giving performance feedback, you should make your feedback and documentation specific and factual, and not base it upon your conclusions, biases, and assumptions. These basic points are covered elsewhere in this book, but here's an example of what this means:

Conclusion	Facts
Your attitude sucks.	*You failed to answer the phone on time five times and arrived late every day.*
You're incompetent.	*You need to learn the new computer program and take a class on project management.*
You're angry.	*You yelled at a customer and slammed the door.*

The people that you manage may not be able to change who they are, but they may change their behavior if you consistently coach and counsel them in the correct way. Most managers wimp out when it comes to giving employees honest and specific feedback. You're not doing them or the organization any favors if you do this, because they'll never improve their performance, and you'll have the headache of dealing with a persistently difficult employee.

Listening to Feedback

Managers often don't want to hear this: You'll never be a successful manager unless you learn how to take feedback from your employees, including negative feedback. You may not like what they have to say, but there's no way to improve your workplace without listening to employee complaints.

For example, I was asked to conduct a team-building session for one of my manufacturing clients. We decide to do an employee survey to find out the issues. The main issue was that the manager refused to hear negative news because she saw her team as "the best team ever." It was an admirable sentiment; however, her attitude ensured that she didn't hear things that she needed to hear, since employees were afraid to bring her problems and interfere with her perception of them.

As a manager, you have certain legal and nonlegal obligations. You aren't legally required to listen to your employees' feedback or complaints. However, it's impossible to get your employees to face their own problem behavior if you won't do the same.

Are You Confrontable?

Are you safe to confront? When I'm asked to coach executives who've been accused of avoiding innovation, abuse, harassment, discrimination, poor conflict management skills, or general "poor people management" skills, they frequently lament: "But I didn't know he or she objected to my behavior. Why didn't they tell me?"

I always respond: "What have *you* done to make it safe for them to come to you and challenge your ideas or complain about your behavior?"

This question is usually followed by silence. The executive views "confrontaphobia" as the other person's problem. But if you feast on conflict like a pit-bull *and* if you're viewed as a person who has power in the organization (these two frequently go hand-in-hand), then you're probably difficult for others to confront. You'll need to take specific steps to make it safer for people to confront you.

One of the best ways to overcome your previous reputation is to be honest about your style. At the next staff meeting, mention that your own awareness has been raised about this issue, and you've realized you may not have been the easiest person to approach with a new idea or conflict. Announce that you've changed your attitude and ask for suggestions about what would make it easier for people to come to you. You might try something like this:

✳   ✳   ✳

I'm becoming increasingly aware of how much I need the feedback of each and every one of you to make this organization a success. I want us to be more innovative and productive. But because I've had a reputation in the past as approaching every conflict or new idea as a personal attack or as an opportunity to debate, I'm realizing that some of you may not have found me approachable. What could I do to make it easier for each of you to come to me with conflicts, feedback, or suggestions?

✳   ✳   ✳

Be prepared for resounding silence.

Your reputation as a pit bull will not be easy to overcome. As one of the high-powered attorneys I coached complained about the associates in his firm: "They won't talk to me; they think I'm the prince of f***ing darkness." If you continue to ask for suggestions about your approachability, however, hints will eventually arrive at your doorstep.

You may ask, "Why do I care?" Many people with an abrasive style have been successful and even gained power in the workplace. Vick, a VP of finance complained when I gave him feedback about his brutal style that had generated a score of employee complaints, saying, "In other organizations, my style would be viewed as an advantage. In fact, I used to receive compliments here for being a tough boss and a hard charger. People today are just too sensitive."

The reality is, the workplace *has* changed. An abrasive style may have been successful yesterday; it will not be successful in the future.

The intervention of the law in workplace management is one obvious reason for the change. The likelihood of an employee charging you with harassment, discrimination, or a violation of the Americans with Disabilities Act (which now may cover psychological as well as physical disabilities) skyrockets if you have a pit-bull reputation. You may protest that you're not discriminating against any particular person, that you treat everyone this way. That argument won't fly with courts or juries. They assume that if you're abusive to everyone, you're even more abusive to people who have less power in the organization—usually women and people of color.

"We need to talk"

According to the Hudson Institute in their *Workforce 2000 Report*, by the year 2000 only 15 percent of new workers will be white males. The demographics of the workplace are changing, and if you don't accept and embrace this fact, you will end up being the one left behind.

Even if you do succeed, you will be stuck with the embarrassing defense of presenting a parade of witnesses to attest to how abusive you were to *them* also.

The second reason you may want to consider changing your pitbull attitude is that with the changing economy, the unpredictable labor market, and the interdependent way most organizations are managed, no one can succeed alone. You'll need the suggestions, dedication, and brainpower of all your people in order to prosper in the future. To elicit the best ideas from your troops, you need to encourage honest feedback.

Many organizations now evaluate both leaders and coworkers based upon how well they address issues such as diversity, consensus, and team building. You can't survive in most organizations without these kinds of skills.

If you're the boss, after announcing at your next meeting your change in attitude, you may want to start having weekly fifteen-minute one-on-one meetings with your direct reports. In those meetings, there should be one item on your agenda—keep asking the questions: *What do you need from me or others to be successful here? What behaviors do I or others engage in that limit your success?*

Again, when you first ask these questions, be prepared for silence. But if you continue to ask these questions week after week, month after month, eventually your colleagues will tell you what they need from you. They'll be more willing to bring you new ideas. More importantly, you will start to see patterns in how others in the organization perceive you and what you must do to change.

You need to keep asking these kinds of questions, not because you're automatically going to change your behavior to suit others, but because you need to be able to skillfully manage their expectations about your behavior. Once you know how they want you to treat them, you can begin to have an honest dialogue about what you can both do differently in the future to make your relationship succeed.

If you're a leader in your organization, consider the model Robert Rodin, president and CEO of Marshall Industries, uses:

*　　*　　*

The more you insist on hearing the truth, and the more often you act on what you've heard, the more often people will give it to you. But most leaders do precisely the opposite. Their companies systematically distort the truth—by design. . . . It's human nature to avoid conflict. . . . If you want to hear criticism, you have to invite it. At least once a month, I convene a forum called "Marshall Live." I gather people at one of our sites: no managers are allowed. I start every meeting by saying something like "This is your company. Tell me what's wrong with it." I get amazing feedback. And then I promise to deal with the feedback in two weeks or less. We don't always do what people want: Companies aren't democracies. But people know that we haven't just heard their criticisms—we've dealt with them.

*　　*　　*

If someone does summon the nerve to complain directly to you about your behavior: Stop. Do not immediately respond. Listen to the suggestion of Jerry Hirshberg:

* * *

Even people who don't mind telling the truth have mixed feelings about hearing the truth. It's like a chemical reaction: Your face goes red, your temperature rises, and you want to strike back. Those are signs of the "two D's": defending and debating. Try to fight back with the "two L's": listening and learning. . . . So the next time you feel yourself defending and debating, stop—and start listening and learning instead. You'll be amazed by what you hear.

* * *

A Step-by-Step Approach

When someone comes to you with a conflict, a new idea, or a criticism about your behavior, follow these steps:

1. **Stop what you're doing and listen.** Give the person your complete attention. If you cannot do that, schedule an appointment as soon as possible.

2. **Do not get defensive.** First, restate what the person said to make sure you understood. Say, for example, "Let me make sure I understand what you said. I heard you say you don't want me to yell at you when I give you feedback. Is that correct?" or "It sounds as if you have a new idea about how to speed up our production schedule."

3. **Apologize if appropriate.** If you're convinced you did nothing wrong, at least say you're sorry your behavior offended them. A good boss or coworker should be sorry someone else is upset even if they're convinced the other person overreacted. If you really did do something very wrong, grovel.

4. **Ask what specific behavior the person needs from you in order to work effectively with you in the future or what their specific idea or request is.** Be certain you focus on behavior, not attitudes or feelings. You can change your own behavior, but you may never be able to change how others feel. Also try to get them to focus on what their specific idea or request is rather than complaints.

5. **Thank them for bringing the matter to your attention and for their courage and honesty.** Let them know you respect and appreciate them for talking with you directly. Unless it's impossible or outrageous, tell them you'll consider their new idea or suggestion.

6. **Follow up.** Make sure you schedule another meeting with them to see if your change in behavior or your response to their idea has met their needs.

7. **Keep talking and keep meeting until your working relationship improves.** If the two of you cannot make it work together, seek an experienced mediator to help you manage your differences.

Does this all sound like too much effort? Unfortunately, there's no quick and easy way to change a pit-bull reputation. You do it by changing your own behavior—inch- by- inch, day- by- day. You also do it by assuming leadership in conflict management in your organization and by encouraging feedback as learning.

How to Manage Your Own Anger

The biggest challenge for most pit-bulls in becoming confrontable may be managing their own anger. *Understanding* your anger is the first step.

The practical popular psychologist Dr. Joyce Brothers, in an interview, summarized the current research about anger management. Understand, she stressed, that your own anger is all about fear, especially the fear of exposing something about yourself and the fear of losing control.

Before exploding from anger, ask yourself of what or whom you are afraid. What might you lose in the encounter? How might you be hurt? Knowing the real, underlying reason may help you control your anger.

Next, suggests Dr. Brothers, don't ignore your anger, but don't express rage inappropriately. There was a time when people thought it healthy to immediately express their anger. More recent research, however, suggests that constant ventilating actually makes us angrier rather than less angry. The most accepted practice is to assume a middle ground between exploding and suppressing anger. Follow these tips, Dr. Brothers suggests:

- Don't ignore your anger, but don't immediately blow up.
- Count to ten.
- Direct your anger at the proper person.
- Deal with the issue at hand; don't bring up old issues.
- Confront the person in private.
- Stay calm; act calm.
- Don't smile—smiling can be viewed as mocking, and can increase anger.
- Use "I" statements, i.e., "I don't want you to throw away my papers without asking," rather than "You have no respect for my things."
- Wait for their explanation.
- Offer understanding (let them save face).

If counting to ten doesn't work, Dr. Brothers suggests you count to 100!

If you can manage your anger so that you're confrontable, and if you encourage skillful confrontation in your own organization, you can move from defending and debating to listening and learning. You can evolve from debate to dialogue. You will have taken another giant step on the road to unleashing the power of a good fight.

Learning to Value the Confrontable Organization

It may be helpful to you and others in your organization to understand just how critical this essential skill is for the future of your organization. Sally Helgesen, author of *The Web of Inclusion: A New Architecture for Building Great Organizations* found in her study that the ability to create open communication where people felt comfortable giving and receiving feedback at all levels of the organization was one of the key predictors of organizational success.

One of my clients, Jane, started her own successful telecommunications company based on this very premise. A long-distance service "re-seller," Jane's company was one of a score of such companies that made their business on the idea of buying long-distance services from the larger telecommunications companies, bundling them in unique ways, and reselling them to individuals. Both Jane and her staff came from various members of the old Bell system.

Accustomed to large, hierarchical organizations, Jane and her staff wanted a change. "We wanted to look like the telecommunications network we were selling. We devised a complex web—like a matrix, really—of interlocking people and departments. We wanted everyone to have access to anyone they needed in the organization.

We wanted everyone's thoughts and ideas so that we would come up with the best solutions to our problems."

One of Jane's first problems was how to design the offices. Breaking with years of Bell tradition, she put her own office out in the open with the other staffers. She toiled at a desk, without walls or even a cube to separate her from her employees. Anyone could talk to her anytime about any concerns. Jane had no secretary and no set schedule. Although this sometimes resulted in a line surrounding her desk, she welcomed the open atmosphere the design created.

"Spontaneous meetings erupted around my desk," Jane told me. "We finally put a couch next to it so that people could participate without fainting from fatigue."

The informal system had another benefit: Rumors were nipped in the bud because anyone who wanted to participate in the initial discussion could. There were no secret meetings behind closed doors. Jane's power as a leader came from the extraordinary openness she was able to demonstrate. Creative solutions flowed out of the chaos surrounding Jane's desk.

Jane also instituted an electronic bulletin board where anyone could post questions about what the company was doing and why. No queries were off-limits. Postings ranged from "Why don't we have a better brand of coffee?" to "Why is our stock down this morning?" Jane, or one of her assistants, answered these queries within forty-eight hours or let the questioner know when the information would be available.

Perhaps most importantly, Jane shaped her successful company by listening and asking the right questions. When anyone would come to her with an issue, her response was always, "What do you think we should do?" Or, "What are your team's ideas for solving that problem?" No one doubted that Jane was anxious to seek out employees' opinions or to be confronted about any issue.

In part because of the depth of inclusion and confrontability, that Jane was able to create, her company survived the recent telecommunications shakedown that plunged many other companies into bankruptcy. When the market tightened, Jane simply solicited the best ideas of all of her employees. Instead of the layoffs other companies had to stomach, Jane asked her people what they should do. When someone suggested offering voluntary three-month sabbaticals to those who wanted them, Jane agreed. Around 15 percent of her employees took advantage of her offer over the next two years; enough to get the company over its financial hump.

Similarly, Southwest Airlines has always created an inclusive culture where employees from vice presidents to baggage handlers knew they could offer suggestions and feedback. Everyone referred to former President, Chairman, and CEO Herb Kelleher as "Herb," and he seemed to know all the employees by their first names. Once, after I gave a speech to their executives, I attempted to walk across the crowded hall with Herb to the buffet table. He stopped so often to ask how someone's divorce was going or to inquire after a new baby that I gave up in starvation and fetched lunch by myself. The next head of Southwest, Coleen Barrett, was also well known for her own encyclopedic knowledge of employee birthdays, anniversaries, and work preferences.

When new employees start at Southwest, they're given a list of 100 questions to answer about the company. Everyone's door—right up to Herb's—is open to these new questioners. From an employee's first moment at Southwest, they know that they can approach anyone with questions or concerns.

What is the benefit of such extraordinary access? While other airlines have been forced into bankruptcy, Southwest has been able to stay their own well-charted course. When other airlines were forced to lay off employees after the September 11 attacks on the World Trade Center and the Pentagon, Southwest instead assured employees that they would stand firm and asked employees to suggest any cost-saving ideas they might have. The strategy worked, and Southwest flew through the storm.

Another one of my clients, a manufacturing company, has always avoided unions in an industry that's largely unionized. "How do they manage this feat?" I once asked the vice president of employee relations. "If you don't want a union," he responded, "act as if you already have one."

Indeed, the company recently fought off an attempted organizing effort by stepping up its normally frenetic schedule of town meetings, management/labor baseball games, and CEO informal lunches with employees, emphasizing access, access, access. The would-be union lost again, gaining only 10 percent of the workers' votes. In addition, profits were up for the third year in a row, running against the industry norm.

Likewise, a large school district in our state was fraught with dissension from teacher unrest, parent unhappiness, and student agitation. When the new superintendent took over, she announced that she was delegating most of her day-to-day duties to one of her deputies. Instead, she would spend her first year "listening and learning." She got an earful.

Teachers wanted more pay and more support. Students wanted open campuses and smoking lounges; parents wanted higher educational standards; and voters wanted better administration accountability. She realized that there was only one way to achieve everyone's objectives: a new bond issue to raise money. The only problem? The past three bond issues had failed miserably.

Continuing to listen to the suggestions from the various stakeholders, she told the voters that she had adopted one citizen group's gutsy idea: The district would receive new money from voters only if they managed to achieve specific educational objectives. No gains, no money. The bond issue passed.

Be Honest and Fair

Being honest comes under the category of "walking the talk." It's difficult to convince employees to do what you say if they don't perceive that you're being straight with them. Although you may not be able to tell them everything you know about what's going on in the organization, you can at least be sincere and honest enough to say that you're sorry but you can't talk about certain things. When you do tell them whatever news you have from the powers that be, they'll be more likely to believe you.

Fairness is a basic requirement of employment law. That means things like giving people accurate and honest performance feedback, warning before termination, and being fair at the time of separation.

The first case in the country to consider this concept was a case brought against Sees Candy Company by a gentleman named Mr. Pugh. He had worked for Sees for thirty-two years, working his way up from the line making candy to vice president. Mr. Pugh and the president socialized and traveled together, along with their wives. The four of them had just returned from a golfing vacation in Spain.

Mr. Pugh walked into the president's office the day after they returned and—out of the blue—the boss said "you're fired." Mr. Pugh had no warning; he'd always thought he was doing well over the course of his thirty-two years.

When Pugh asked why, the president said: "Look deep within your heart and you will find the answer." Mr. Pugh looked deep within his heart and found the name of an employment attorney, sued, and won.

The court found that firing to be a violation of the "covenant of good faith and fair dealing," which is implied in most employment contracts in most states. It basically means you have to be fair.

You'll learn more about the concept of fairness in managing your employees in other parts of this book.

Manager's Role

Additional requirements of your role as a manager are the following:

- You have a fiduciary duty to the organization.
- You have to keep employee matters confidential—only people who need to know should know.
- You have an obligation to coach, communicate, and help people succeed.

We'll explore these topics later, but essentially a fiduciary obligation means that you have to give your loyalty to the organization and protect it. This doesn't mean that you should ever do anything illegal or unethical, but if there's a conflict or a disagreement between an employee and the company, you have to back the company. You can, of course, push back and let your management know that you disagree with whatever decision they've made about an employee, but if you lose that battle, you should not let the employee know that you disagree as a way of seeming friendlier to the employee. Ultimately, of course, if you disagree too often with your organization, or you keep trying to persuade them to change and they don't listen to you, you may need to work elsewhere. Constantly badmouthing your own employer, however, to your employees, will not serve you or them.

Confidentiality means that you keep employee matters limited to people who need to know. This is generally a smaller group than most managers might think. Just because someone else is a manager or supervisor in your company doesn't mean that he or she needs to know about an employee matter.

Finally, a part of fairness is helping employees succeed. You need to coach and communicate with employees. The law requires you to be fair, and a part of fairness is helping the people who work for you learn and grow. You can't just throw them into the lake and take a "sink or swim" attitude.

Grounding Yourself Before Talking with an Employee

You'll find dozens of other examples of specific, challenging conversations with employees throughout this book, but all of them are grounded in the basic rights, roles, and responsibilities of this chapter. When you decide to take a stand with an employee, be sure that you're starting from the place outlined here. Otherwise, your attempt to communicate will very likely be out of bounds.

Sample Script

SANDRA: Jake, I need to talk to you.

JAKE: Yea, what?

SANDRA: I've noticed that you've been arriving at 11:00 and leaving at 3:00 every day. Even though we have flextime, you're required to be here every day during our core hours, between 10:00 and 4:00. (Reminding him that he has to show up on time.)

JAKE: Well, I've just been really busy with this other project I've been doing at home so I haven't been getting much sleep.

SANDRA: I respect your right to do whatever you want on your own time but you do have to show up for work here on time. (Reminding him that employees owe their primary duty of loyalty to the company.) If you can't do that, I'm going to have to put you on a performance plan. I need you to consider this as a verbal warning.

JAKE: Well, my last manager didn't seem to care.

SANDRA: That may be but I'm your manager now and I have different standards. (Recognizing her right to change standards.) Also, I'll need you to e-mail me your understanding of this conversation so that I'm sure we're both on the same page. (Requests follow-up by e-mail.)

JAKE: Okay.

Employee Conversation Don'ts	Employee Conversation Dos
Wimp out.	Learn and stand for your rights as a manager.
Be unfair.	Consider fairness.
Do what the last manager did.	Realize you can change standards.
Fail to communicate.	Give employee feedback.
Refuse to listen.	Listen to their feedback.

"We need to talk"

Chapter 2

How to Talk about Poor Performance

GRACE KETTERING STARED out the window of her office toward the "pit," the group of telephone sales reps that she managed. Much to her amazement, out of her twelve reps, most actually did a good job, remaining enthusiastic while cold calling and trying to sell new phone service. But two reps had problems: late attendance, poor phone skills, and a lack of initiative. She'd talked and talked with them to no avail. Now she needed to up the ante.

The problem was that she had no idea what to say.

Setting Objectives

As explained in Chapter 1, from the first day forward, you need to set concrete and specific goals and objectives so that your employees know what's expected and have them e-mail back to you their understanding of what you want. These objectives should be behaviorally specific: something that they can say or do. If it's not something that they can say or do, then it's not specific enough. Check out the following examples:

Vague	Behaviorally Specific
Use good phone skills.	*Follow the written script.*
Have a good attitude.	*Show up on time; meet your daily call goals.*
Be persistent.	*Ask for the sale at least three times.*

If you have not set forth these kinds of behaviorally specific goals and objectives, you will find that it's very difficult to manage poor performance. It's much easier for employees to exhibit quality work if they know specifically what you think good work looks like. It's much easier to create good performance if your workers have a clear vision in their own minds of what you're trying to accomplish.

Of course, this requires you to do something that many managers have trouble accomplishing: having a clear vision themselves of their own goals and objectives. If you're not crystal clear about this in your own mind, you'll find it difficult for employees to do the same.

Again, before you deal with poor performance, you should have clearly stated goals and objectives and follow up by having employees e-mail their understanding of what you said. This allows you to make sure that they understand what you're trying to say to them.

If you have not done this before, the first step in managing poor performance is to start now.

One-on-Ones That Work

You will need to follow the standard management mantra of "praising in public and criticizing in private." Find a quiet office or corner of the plant or shop and make sure that your conversation cannot be overheard. No one likes to have their private business spread out all over the workplace and, in general, performance problems and other employee personnel issues should be kept confidential anyway.

Use this model:

- **Clarify the performance issue.**
- **Outline the problem by getting straight to the point.** Don't leave the employee wondering or hanging around trying to imagine what you're talking about.
- **Be specific.** Follow the examples above of behaviorally specific ways of acting and being. Employees cannot realistically respond to vague directives.
- **Ask the employee what they think about what you've said and listen.** Don't, however, get distracted from your main message if the employee starts dodging and weaving and offering a lot of excuses that you know are nutty.
- **Repeat what the employee needs to do to improve.** Repetition, repetition, repetition is the key here.
- **PIP or e-mail back.** If your organization has a formal performance improvement plan (PIP) then you need to follow that structure and make sure that you dot all i's and cross all t's. If

not, you can use the technique from Chapter 1, and instruct the employee to e-mail back to you their understanding of what you want them to do. Again, be prepared to have to go through several iterations before you get this one right.

- **Set a follow-up meeting, sometime soon.** One week would be appropriate for some workplaces, but certainly no later than one month.
- **Be sure to document all steps in this process in your own management file.** What to document? Just the facts—not your opinions, conclusions, or assumptions.

Here are some more specifics about these steps.

Clarifying Performance Issues

Before you can accurately tell the employee how you see his or her performance, you need to clarify the performance issue for yourself. Clarifying the performance issue is vital to developing a solution and change of behavior in the employee. You and the employee need to perceive the situation in the same way and agree on what the issue might be.

One of the best ways to clarify the issue with the employee is to ask the employee some open-ended questions to understand the issue from his or her perspective.

Examples of some questions you could ask are as follows:

- Tell me what are some of the skills you don't think you're using?
- What would you like to be doing?
- What might you be able to do differently to help this situation?

Once you understand, paraphrase the information back to make sure you're on the same page. Use close-ended questions.

Open-ended questions are those that cannot be answered with a simple yes-or-no answer. They require the employee to elaborate and explain.

Close-ended questions can be responded to in short or one-word answers. First, paraphrase what the employee has said, and then, respond with a close-ended question, such as the following:

- Did I understand you correctly?
- What I heard you saying was this. . . . Do I understand the situation as you do?

Clarifying the situation from the employee's perspective doesn't mean that you're going to agree with the employee. It just means that it will be easier to get employees fully invested in what you're saying if they feel that you've really listened to them. You may have to "agree to disagree" about what's going on with their performance, but there can be great power in making sure that the employee feels really listened to and understood.

In addition, it's always important to manage the employee's expectations. So many managers are afraid to find out what their employees expect because they feel that they may have to actually meet their employees' perspective. Not true. You don't have to do what employees expect, but if you don't know what they expect it can be difficult, if not impossible, to manage those expectations.

Documentation Dos and Don'ts

When you're managing performance problems, documentation is key. The problem is, you're already documenting all the time so some of the key is to keep the documentation that you already have and to avoid accidental documentation.

What kind of documentation are you already making?

- Internal memos, letters
- E-mails
- Notes of meetings, calls
- Progress reports
- Division/department employee rankings
- One-on-one agendas
- Employee self-appraisals
- Rework orders
- Warnings and corrective action
- Performance improvement plans
- Web pages
- Instant messaging

Where Is Your Current Documentation?

Whether you like it or not, your documentation is already saved on your hard drives and servers, personnel files, PCs, laptops, pagers, calendars, time records, cell phones, expense reports, and more.

Some electronic minefields include things like admissions. If you say in an e-mail to HR: "Gee, think that I just did something illegal," that's a dangerous admission. Also, avoid emotional comments and sarcasm, which may not come out the same way in writing.

> **"We need to talk"**
>
> What is accidental documentation? Things like emotional outbursts that might include unprofessional comments toward an employee or electronic versions of rough drafts of employee memos (which should be written on paper and then destroyed). E-mail, computer files, and web visit logs are admissible in court, belong to the employer, are not private to you or any employee, and may be accessed at any time. Beware!

When you're documenting performance or other problems, you need to follow all your employer's policies and procedures and assume that a judge or your boss is reading your e-mail. Don't e-mail employee problems to HR or management. Call instead. If you e-mail them something emotional, that could blow up later in court. So just call HR and talk to them. At some point you may be communicating back and forth though e-mail, but first, you need to talk.

Talking Before Documentation

Now, of course, documenting should not be the first step in managing performance; talking should always be the first step. Sometimes, however, when you're coaching an employee a warning sign starts going off, and you just know (if you've been managing for some time) that this might turn into a bigger problem.

When that happens, in addition to having a conversation and having them e-mail back to you their understanding, you want to write a brief note to jog your memory about the conversation. I call the total of these informal notes your "manager's file." For one thing, these notes shouldn't be kept only when there's a problem; you should also put notes of good things or specific conversations in there to jog your memory.

Performance Improvement Plans

In addition to performance appraisals (which we'll cover in the next chapter) a key document is the performance improvement plan (PIP). It's critical that you follow all your organization's policies and procedures. And you should take a gradual, step-by-step approach. If you have an employee who last year you rated highly and this year you want to rate much lower, and there's no documentation or PIP in between, that looks highly suspicious. So, instead of a big drop, throw-them-off-the-cliff approach, use a stair-step approach. Say, "You're doing great here. Like to see some improvement here, and I'm sure you'll do it." Next time, "Still want to see some improvement here." Next time, and so on, all the way down, so that when they get the bad appraisal, they're not surprised. Performance appraisals should always be "no surprises."

Performance Improvement Process

When you do decide that you need performance to improve, follow this checklist:

- What is the employee doing—or not doing—that affects *job performance?* What is the impact of this behavior on team performance and how does that relate to the needs of your organization?

- If there's no impact on individual or group performance, *stop*! If the employee is having a personal issue, refer the employee to your employee assistance program or some other outside resource. A good thing to say anytime someone has a performance problem is this: "If there's anything that I'm doing or that anyone else at work is doing that's interfering with your performance or success, please let me know. If there's something that's going on in your personal life that's interfering with your performance, that's none of my business but we do have employee assistance (or other outside resource) so you may want to contact them."

- If you have identified a performance problem, then consider the following:

1. Does the employee have a clear understanding of what you and the company expect?
2. Are expectations consistent across the team?
3. Are you treating this employee consistently with others?
4. Does the employee have the time, tools, training, and support needed to perform?
5. Does the employee have the technical and behavioral skills needed?
6. Are there special issues to consider (disability, family member illness, religious observance, etc.)?
7. Decide what you want the employee to do.
8. Create an action plan and timeline.
9. Discuss with the employee and get feedback.
10. Document, document, document. (Correctly, of course!)

Write Objective Documentation

When you are finally ready to write your documentation, you want to make sure that you write objective documentation. Here are some tips:

- Be honest! You're not doing employees any favors by not being honest. There's no way they can improve if you don't give them the valid feedback that they need.
- Be specific. Limit to objective, verifiable facts. How do you know if a fact is verifiable? It must have sensory detail—there's something in there that you saw or heard. If someone came to you and told you something, that's something that you heard. Just write it down in quotes, along with the source.
- Use clear, precise language. Be specific.
- Do not give your conclusions without facts and examples to back you up. You can base them on reports from witnesses if you judge them to be reliable.
- Avoid sarcasm and demeaning comments.

If you want to shape behavior in order to create results consistent with a performance plan or to deal with any issue that has the potential to be emotionally charged, try the 1-2-3-Go! approach. Here's how it works:

1. Say something that implies understanding or appreciation.
2. Make a behaviorally specific (doable) request. (It has to be something the person can do or say, or it's not behaviorally specific.)
3. Add more appreciation and understanding.
4. Go away; do not nag, hover, or whine.

Examples of vague requests vs. specific behavior-based changes:

Vague	Specific
Stop bothering Miranda!	Miranda can't work when you're at her desk talking. Please stop.
Don't be rude to callers.	Greet each caller. Ask how you can help them.
Don't harass the women.	Please don't make comments about your colleague's physical appearance.

When trying to shape problem behavior, you can and should repeat this request three times, unless it's something that's clearly unethical or illegal or a clear violation of your policies. After the third time, you need to add consequences if you expect the behavior to change.

Here's how it works.

1. **Appreciation or understanding.** "I know how much you like to use your speaker phone, and I appreciate that sometimes you remember not to do that when Miranda's working. I understand how hard it can be to change a habit."

2. **Specific behavioral request.** "I need you to remember not to use it at all when Miranda's in the office. Please talk on the phone instead."

3. **Add consequence.** "I'm sorry to have to take this step, but if it happens again, I'm going to have to put a written warning in your file. Miranda simply can't get her work done when you do this."

4. **Appreciation and understanding.** "Thank you. Again, I know how hard it can be to change and I appreciate you taking these steps."

5. Go! Walk away. Do not nag, complain, or whine.

If the behavior doesn't change or improve, you will need to escalate. The biggest mistake in this process is to delineate consequences and then not pull the trigger. It turns a consequence into an empty threat. When you implement the consequence, use the same 1-2-3-Go! format. It's your problem, and you need to find a way to deal with it.

"We need to talk"

You'll notice that all these are worded as requests, not complaints. While you need to outline the way you see the person's problem behavior as suggested above, it's a mistake just to complain without a specific request. And yet this is what many managers actually do. They just complain and do not request, which is 100-percent ineffective. Master the art of making specific requests instead of complaints, and you'll find your performance problems much more solvable.

Appropriate consequences might be discipline, up to and including termination. You do need to warn someone if something could lead to termination if his or her behavior doesn't change; otherwise, you're not treating the employee fairly.

Harnessing the Art of Inquiry

We live in an age when we need to involve those we lead in order to accomplish our goals. In order to gain their buy-in, we need to learn how to *inquire* instead of just informing them of what we're doing. Notice how much more effective questions, rather than orders, are in the following examples:

Orders	Questions
Here's the schedule for completing this project.	*What are your ideas for a workable schedule for this project?*
Here's what I need from you to accomplish this.	*What are you willing to do to accomplish our goals?*
You need to get along with X.	*There seems to be something X does that sets you off. What might that be?*
You need to meet deadlines.	*There seems to be something in the way of you meeting deadlines. What might that be?*

The most effective questions after a mishap are "What did we *learn* from this?" and "What did we *learn* today?" Start practicing the Art of Inquiry. You'll find the process an effective leadership tool to add to your arsenal.

Specific Examples of Problem Performance and How to Talk about Them

Late Attendance. Lisa, you've been late ten times this month. We've talked about this several times and you say that you will change but you haven't. What's in the way of making this change?

Sloppy Work. Anthony, the last document you sent me had thirty typos. You know that we need client documents to be accurate. What ideas do you have about how to make this happen?

Disrespectful Behavior. Sandy, when you spoke to Jim just now I noticed that you were yelling and using profanity. You know that's not acceptable under our code of conduct. How can we make sure that you follow our rules in the future and talk with people in a respectful way?

Lack of Enthusiasm. Cheri, I noticed that you seem to be following up with client calls late and not returning some at all. You know that we're supposed to return all client calls within twenty-four hours. How can we make sure that this happens?

Argumentative Employee. Sam, it seems that every time I announce a new company rule, you decide to argue about it.

I realize that you don't agree with many things that the company is doing and I'm willing to listen to your ideas but at some point, you have to get behind what we've decided and make your peace with it. How can we make that happen?

Underperformer. Julie, we've had several conversations about how you're not meeting your sales goals but it's still not happening. What else do you think you need from us to make sure that you make your numbers?

Check for Strengths Mismatch

Sometimes, despite all your attempts to improve performance, an employee refuses to come up to snuff. In that situation, you need to check for a strengths mismatch.

We all have strengths and weaknesses. Much of employee management focuses on correcting employee weaknesses and trying to move them up to where they need to be for performance. Yet sometimes, despite perfect one-on-ones, follow-up e-mails, clarifying the issue, and asking for change, the employee's performance stubbornly refuses to budge. In that situation, you need to check for strengths mismatch.

What this means is that the employee may be totally mismatched for the job.

In recent years, there's been a lot of research that supports the idea of focusing on strengths rather than weaknesses.

Generally, when a task matches our strength, we feel energized and excited. When we're doing work that requires us to use a skill set that we may have trouble with, we feel drained. While every job has draining tasks for any given person, if employees are spending too much time on tasks that drain rather than energize, your chances of ever bringing their performance up to the level you need are slim.

When you're tearing your hair out over a performance problem, you might try having the employee keep track of their time over the period of a week. Ask them to note the times they feel particularly happy and energized in their job, and the time when they find their work most draining. Then use that analysis to have a frank conversation with the employee about whether the job they're in will ever match up with their strengths. If not, you may need to reassign them, redesign the job, or ultimately, gently move them out the door.

The Key to Managing Poor Performance

This chapter contains many tips on managing poor performance, but the overarching idea you should bear in mind is that you need to *manage*. As outlined in Chapter 1, managers have many reasons for thinking that they don't have the time for tough conversations: lack of time, lack of energy, fear of losing a friend or starting a fight, and lawsuit paranoia. None of these excuses will save you when faced with an employee who needs you.

Yes, employees need you. New employees or employees who are having performance problems need frequent—preferably daily—contact with you. All the research on younger workers (the so-called Generation X or Y and Millennial Generations) points to the idea that the best and the brightest of that group have been raised by parents, teachers, and coaches who constantly gave them feedback and coaching. They expect, need, and thrive on it.

While someone from an older generation might resent all this intrusion and long for a more "hands-off" attitude, the younger workers will most likely expect your "face time" and feel neglected if they don't get it. If you're managing remotely, you need to have as many phone conversations as you can manage. So if you have a younger worker who seems to have lost her enthusiasm, the key may be to increase the amount of time you're spending with her and use all the techniques you've learned in this chapter to manage her performance: e-mailing confirmations of your conversations with her, using requests not complaints, asking open-ended questions, and harnessing the power of inquiry.

The new workplace benefits much more from a fluid, day-to-day negotiation of an employee's duties and responsibilities. The old model of once-a-year evaluations fails in this work environment. What managers must do is aggressively manage good performance before it morphs into performance problems. This requires more managing to results, instead of face time or busy-work. Managers need to know how they will measure the results of good performance and give employees frequent feedback about whether they're reaching these goals, rather than waiting until bad performance erupts. Then the manager must engage in crisis management.

Frequently, managing results rather than face time or clock-punching requires a great deal of creativity from managers. Managers need to use praise and face time as rewards, as well as rewarding employees with assignments and work environments, flextime, and other nonmonetary perks. (Not that a surprise cash bonus isn't a good idea, but frequently managers today simply don't have those bonuses to hand out.)

Workplace studies have shown that nothing affects an employee's performance, loyalty to the organization, or desire to stay more than his or her relationship with their immediate supervisor.

It's well worth your time and effort to make sure that yours is a good one.

Sample Script

GRACE: Terry, I need to talk to you about your performance.

TERRY: Yes?

GRACE: You don't seem to be meeting your daily goals anymore. (States the problem clearly.) I'm wondering what's going on from your perspective? (Asks open-ended questions.)

TERRY: I don't know. I just don't seem to have any enthusiasm anymore.

GRACE: I see that. What do you think would make that change?

TERRY: I'm not really sure what to do.

GRACE: Well, we need to find a way to help you improve. Is there any part of your job that you enjoy?

TERRY: I don't like making cold calls at all anymore. What I do like is the follow-up calls for existing customers.

GRACE: Interesting. Well, here's what I'd like you to do. Keep a log all week of which activities you do that help increase your enthusiasm and which do not. I'd like to find out what gives you energy at work. (Checking for strengths mismatch.) Here's a form I've used in the past for this kind of analysis. I'm not sure that we can meet your needs with this job, but as a first step, I'd like to find out where you're at.

TERRY: Great, I'll try it.

Employee Conversation Don'ts	Employee Conversation Dos
Be vague.	*Be specific.*
Fail to document.	*Document specifics.*
Document accidently.	*Document correctly.*
Complain.	*Make specific requests.*
Order around.	*Use inquiry.*
Give up on performance.	*Increase face time.*
Focus exclusively on employees' weaknesses.	*Find their strengths.*

Chapter 3

How to Talk During Challenging Performance Reviews

RYAN ADAMS REREAD the performance review he'd written and scowled. Max was one of the most difficult people in his department. He was constantly griping and complaining about something. Ryan had no choice but to give him a "does not meet expectations" on his performance review form. He knows that Max is going to hit the roof and start spouting off about how Ryan is unfair.

The only problem is that Ryan has absolutely no idea what to say!

Performance Appraisal Checklist

While the focus of this chapter is to address challenging performance appraisals, first we will review the basics. If you don't have these down, *every* performance review will be difficult.

First, you need to center yourself in the concept that the purpose of a performance review is to help your employees learn and grow. While it can be easy to think that the only purpose is to satisfy HR or legal, or just to "get it done" so that it's not hanging over your head, the reality is that there's much more at stake. One of your jobs as a manager is to coach people, mentor them, and help them succeed. Ideally, performance reviews should be a useful tool to these ends.

Performance reviews are key legal and management documents. You need to do them . . . and on time! Managers frequently procrastinate when it comes to these pesky tasks, and that doesn't serve them or the employees. Nothing makes an employee angrier than not having a performance review for years and then suddenly finding him- or herself in deep trouble. It's not fair to blindside people with a poor performance review.

As a practical matter, you should give appraisals after three months, six months, and then yearly on the anniversary of the hire date.

Before you do this year's appraisal, look at last year's. If the employee has shown improvement over the year, note that. If the performance has deteriorated, say so. If the performance appraisal this year is significantly different from last year's, say why.

If another manager wrote the last performance appraisal, your ratings may be very different. Employees who have worked under the same manager for years learn to do their jobs in a certain manner. When new managers come in, or when current managers take training courses, they often want to change old ways of doing things. Be sure to make a note about a difference in standards on the appraisal form. For example, you may write, "Your last manager rated you excellent even though you were 85 percent of quota. I rate employees excellent only if they reach 125 percent of quota."

As long as you have a legitimate business reason, you can change performance standards.

You can also change employees' job responsibilities. You must inform them clearly of the new job requirements, either in the performance appraisal or other written memo. You also must give them time to achieve the new goals. As long as the assignments are achievable by a reasonable person, you can implement your changes—even if your particular employees can't achieve them.

For appraisals to be accurate, the form itself must be fair. A good performance appraisal documents your management efforts for the employee over the year. It summarizes the results of the past year and plans for the next.

If an overall rating is given, you should not just average the scores of the different categories. You should weigh the relative importance of the various categories to different jobs. For example, initiative is very important for a manager, whereas good work habits are almost assumed. The relative importance of these categories might be the opposite for an assembler.

When you do sit down to do reviews, follow these rules:

- **Be prepared.** Don't do them at the last minute. Take the time and energy to do them well. Your employees try to give you their best work (well, at least most of them), and you owe them this attention and feedback.
- **Document and collect e-mail confirmations all year.** As we discussed in the preceding chapters, if you follow this format, you'll find that your employees have done a lot of your work for you and you can use this e-mail trail to start drafting the performance review itself.

- **Be honest.** Managers have a hard time being honest on performance reviews. You're not doing anyone any favors by sugarcoating the truth. Remember, the purpose of a performance review is to help people to learn and grow. No one learns and grows without adequate and honest feedback. Emphasize to your employees that you will be giving all employees honest reviews in order to help them improve their performance. It will prepare them to hear that they have areas where they can improve, as well as help to keep you focused on being honest and fair.

- **Be specific.** Again, this is an area where most managers fail. Use the tips on documentation and specifics from the preceding chapters.

- From the first day on,

1. Set goals keyed to organizational strategy and job description;
2. Establish standards keyed to performance appraisal;
3. State how those standards will be measured;
4. Monitor progress with regular one-on-ones;
5. Revise and set goals; and
6. Document the process with follow-up memos or e-mails.

Additional things that you should be doing in every performance review include the following:

- Compare this year to last year. If there's been a big drop in performance, you should be investigating why this happened and do what it takes to improve their performance. If there's a big improvement over last year, you should be giving the employee a big pat on the back and "well done."

- Include strengths and areas of improvement. As mentioned previously, everyone should have a mixture of these, even your best (or worst) employees.

- Avoid the halo or devil effect. What does this mean? Some people make an initial great impression and then can do no wrong. Others have the opposite problem. We're all a mixture of the light and the dark: It's good to recognize that on reviews and not get mesmerized in either direction.

- Appraise the entire year. Nothing makes an employee angrier than if they've done a good job of working for most of the year and then messed up last month and you just focus on that.

- Provide specific examples. We've already covered this several times, but perhaps you're beginning to see how important this one is!

- Focus on behavior and results.

- Don't focus on attitude and personalities.

- Do be sure to ask for feedback and listen after you give them a review.

- If you're asking them to improve, be sure to ask: What's in it for them? Why should they want to improve? What motivation can you provide for them to do this?

- Avoid mentioning protected characteristics (age, race, gender, etc.) and medical or disability leave taken.

- Keep reviews and other performance or misconduct issues confidential. Only people who *need* to know should know. This generally does not include other managers who are your peers or other employees. If you're dealing with a sticky situation, you may want to ask your manager, HR, legal, or another expert for advice but talking to other managers—except in a highly theoretical way—should be entirely off-limits.

- Schedule follow-up meetings and goals. Employees are more likely to improve if they know they have a meeting coming up where they're likely to be held accountable.

The Importance of Performance Appraisals in Legal Matters

Performance appraisals are a critical document in every employment lawsuit. They can make or break your case. Appraisals should tell the story of the employee's life with the company and should be given regularly to create a complete picture of the employee's job history.

Sometimes appraisals show years of substandard performance. If the employee continued to receive pay increases, it will appear that you condoned it. And it will be difficult for you to justify termination for poor performance if you've put up with it for long. If the employee was so bad, why didn't you terminate before? Appraisals should answer these questions, or better still, never raise them.

Self-evaluations

Some managers like to have employees fill out the appraisal themselves, to see their self-evaluation. Considering the employee's point of view is a good way to show you treat employees fairly. It also is useful in deciding how to rate the employee. If you do accept employee self-appraisals, keep them with yours in the personnel file.

Self-evaluations do not mean you have to accept the employee's version of the facts. If the employee is accurate, acknowledge that. But don't back down from a poor review if one is warranted. Some employees like to inflate their results, assuming that you will want to avoid the conflict of telling them they're wrong. Don't let this happen to you.

You can always acknowledge their different perception and work toward helping them understand that your perspective is simply different. You don't need to agree with their view, but you do need to know what their view is so that you can manage their expectations. They may think that your perception of their performance may be wrong, silly, or stupid but ultimately, you are the boss.

If you do decide to have your employees fill out their own form, it's a good idea to make sure that they cover such things as their goals and objectives for the next six months, the next year, and the next five years. You should be asking all employees these kinds of questions. If you ask all employees, you're well within your rights to ask the same questions of employees you think may be pregnant, may be leaving, or may have other issues. The problem comes when you only ask some employees but not others.

An employee's view of his performance can be especially helpful if you've failed to keep up with him during the course of the year. Sometimes, you may not even be aware of all the projects he's working on. If this is the case, his review of his own performance can help you get up-to-date without revealing that you don't know something that he probably thinks you should.

If you do ask or allow employees to fill out their own forms, be sure that you do them the courtesy of reading it and commenting on what they've written. It can be very demoralizing to an employee if you don't read their input. They frequently spend a great deal of time on these forms and expect you to read and consider seriously what they've written.

Key Points in Dealing with Difficult Performance Reviews

By now, you understand that the performance appraisal process is part of an ongoing year-round process of giving constant feedback and support, making sure people know what is expected, and setting goals for the future. However, understanding the performance appraisal process in theory and actually sitting across from an employee and following through are two very different things. If employees always behaved the way they do in theoretical books, life would be easy. Unfortunately, people don't always respond predictably, and knowing how to handle difficult performance appraisal situations is imperative for holding onto good employees and gently transitioning poor performers out of the organization to someplace where (you hope) they'll be a better fit.

For just these situations, I've developed key points that you'll need to remember. I've given this system the (perhaps corny) acronym HAPPY, with the hope that it will be easy to remember and that it will lead to at least happier, if not happy, reviews. These are the key points to hold onto as you're talking with a difficult employee about a challenging review:

- Honestly tell the employee exactly how you see the performance situation.

- Ask for feedback about what you've said and listen to the employee's response.
- Partner with the employee to find the solution.
- Persist until the change you've requested happens.
- Remember *why* you do performance reviews (to help people learn and grow) and ask yourself why the employee would want to improve. (What's in it for him or her?)

In the next sections, we'll drill down on each of these in order to flesh out how to do each one.

Honestly Tell the Employee What You Think

First, you need to be sure that you have a clear understanding of what the problem is. Have you honestly assessed what the problem is, come up with specifics that are "doable" and behaviorally specific? If not, you need to go back to preparation. You should come into the session well prepared to explain what the problem is and why it's important to your organization's goals, values, and success. If it's not affecting individual or team performance relating to these goals and objectives, *stop!* You need to ask yourself some hard questions about why you're even raising this issue.

Ask for Feedback

Once you've given your honest, specific assessment of the problem, you need to sit back and listen. Be prepared for the employee to be angry, argumentative, or in denial. At this stage, you just want to listen. Sometimes allowing the employee to voice all their feelings and concerns can be very therapeutic for them, even if you're not agreeing with what they've said.

> ## "We need to talk"
>
> In our fast-paced, overstimulating age, having someone's total attention can be a gift. Give them the gift of really listening, and you may be surprised by what they say. Keep asking open-ended questions, as discussed in Chapter 2, until they've been allowed to say everything they need to, you can be sure that they've run out of steam, and you really know what their concerns and opinions might be. Again, this isn't because you're going to change their review or do what they want, it's just because you're going to focus on their needs so that, down the line, you can manage—not agree with or meet—their expectations.

Listening is one of the hardest skills to learn. Here's an effective listening checklist to help you see whether you have effective listening skills:

- Don't use roadblocks that stop people from talking, such as
    - Unsolicited Advice: "You should speak to your spouse about it."
    - Hostile "Why" Questions: "Why did you do that?"
    - Dismissive Encouragement: "You'll feel better about it tomorrow."
    - Unnecessary Criticizing: "If you hadn't procrastinated . . . ."
    - Constant Interruptions: "That's nothing. Listen to this . . . ."
    - Related Stories: "I had the same experience last year."

- Continue to ask open-ended questions to get the whole story:
    - "What happened next?"
    - "What was your reaction?"

- Summarize employees' statements so they know you've heard them.
  - ➤ "So you believe that . . . ?"
  - ➤ "What you are saying is . . . ."

- Ask "what next" questions so they discover their own answers:
  - ➤ "What have you done to resolve the problem?"
  - ➤ "What else do you think could be done?"
  - ➤ "What have others tried in similar situations that worked?"

Partner with the Employee to Find a Solution

Partnering is an approach to conflict that tries to put two or more people on the same team while putting the problem on the opposite team. You and the employee are not enemies. In this model, you are just two people jointly trying to solve a problem.

Although it is imperative to have the employee involved in determining the solution to a performance problem, it can be helpful to have a few options to suggest if the employee is unsure of how to fix the problem. Keep in mind that the employee needs to be part of the decision as to which solution works best for him.

Persist Until Things Change

Persistence pays off in many areas of life, and managing difficult performance situations is no exception. The main action managers can take to encourage employees to follow through is to set a follow-up meeting with an employee. The follow-up meeting shows the employee you care and also gives her a timeline of what is expected. It's also an excellent way to hold the employee accountable for her behavior. When the employee knows that there is an additional meeting scheduled to discuss her progress, she has a vested interest in making sure some progress has taken place.

Other ways to make sure that employees take action would be to suggest they take a specific class, read a certain book, or listen to a related CD in order for them to learn the skills they need. Then, they can report back to you about what they've learned. You could also require them to install and use performance management software if time management is an issue, or assign a mentor who has mastered the skill or task that they need assistance handling in order to help them learn what they need.

You might also have the employee create an action plan of what he is going to do, resources he will need to follow through, and when he plans on completing each activity.

How long you should give your employee to improve depends on what he is doing incorrectly and how much it is affecting the business. If it's misconduct—theft, severe harassment, or the like—obviously he may be fired immediately. If it's some other kind of performance issue, a general guideline is to give the employee whatever amount of time you would give a new person to learn a new task or job.

Longer-term employees should be given more time since, presumably, the reason you've kept them around so much is that they've earned a certain amount of tenure and respect. Furthermore, the courts always give a lot of deference to long-term employees.

Why *Are You Doing This?*

Throughout this communication process, it's important to remember the underlying reasons why you're doing this. Performance reviews—even difficult ones—are meant to help people learn and grow. Also, remember that you need to provide employees with "why" in order to get them to improve their performance. They need to know and understand why they would even want to do such a thing.

Important Keys to Success

In the HAPPY model, perhaps the most important thing to remember is that you must first clarify the issue with the employee. If you can figure out what is *really* going on and why, then you can usually help the employee figure out how to move forward. The number-one mistake managers make when dealing with employee issues is that managers may assume that they know what is causing employees' problems instead of asking employees what is going on and trying to see the situation from an employee's perspective. It's also critical to include the employee as a partner when determining solutions to the performance problem because if the employee takes part in creating the solution, she is more motivated to achieve it.

In All Things, Be Fair

One of the hallmarks of employment law (in most states) as well as good management is to treat employees fairly. This is especially important when you're dealing with a difficult performance appraisal. Essentially, the courts have determined that every contract, including the basic employment contract, contains an implied covenant. A covenant is simply one section of a contract. This section requires the employer to treat the employee fairly. It's called the *covenant of good faith and fair dealing.*

Once you accept the idea that every employee has a contract, it makes sense to require employers to treat employees fairly. In other contexts, the courts have said that if the parties to a contract are in an unequal bargaining position, the weaker party should be protected from the stronger one.

> **"We need to talk"**
>
> In the employment area, employees generally are the weaker parties. They have very little say about the amount of pay they receive, the kinds of work they do, and their working conditions.

In the past, it was thought that if employees didn't like the working conditions, they could just "vote with their feet" and go to work elsewhere. But in recent years, the courts have recognized that requiring employees to leave creates a hardship for them, particularly as they get older. So, gradually, in most states, the courts have concluded that employers should treat employees fairly.

Ideally, managers help employees achieve success. They treat the employment relationship as an ongoing process of constant communication, accurate feedback, and gentle correction. They give positive reinforcement. They take the time to be good coaches.

Fortunately for those of us humans who become managers, the law does not require us to be ideal. Although there is a lot of language in their opinions about fairness, the courts have actually required fairness only in a few limited situations. One of the main ones is in evaluating performance.

Once you think that you understand the situation from the employee's perspective, it is important to paraphrase—not parrot—the information back to the employee to make sure that you're both on the same page. Paraphrasing is where you add something to or rephrase what the employee has said in such a way as to demonstrate that you've really heard and processed what he has to say. (Simply repeating what he said would be parroting.)

Examples of Asking for the Employee's Perspective on the Situation

Here are some examples of various typical scenarios and some open-ended questions you could ask to help clarify the issue with the employee.

situation 1: You have a performance review tomorrow with Carol, one of your best employees. Lately, Carol has been coming in to work at least twenty minutes late and taking an extra half-hour for lunch. You have discussed this with her before, but she is still showing up late. What can you ask Carol to help you understand what is going on?

situation 1 suggested questions: Carol, you have been doing an outstanding job with meeting your job requirements—in fact, you have really exceeded my expectations. You give 110 percent in every area. My one concern is that you are consistently late in the morning and coming back from lunch. We have discussed this before; what do you feel is the problem?

situation 2: Bob's ninety-day performance review is coming up. He has only been with the company for three months, and he has never really shown any interest in his job. He seems apathetic toward his job and toward the other people he works with. What can you ask Bob to help you understand what is going on?

*situation **2** suggested questions:* Bob, you have been with us for ninety days now, and from my perspective, you don't seem very interested in your job. Would you share your perspective with me about how you feel about your job?

*situation **3**:* Adam told you last week that he was getting a divorce. He has been slacking off for the last six months. You have tried to discuss it with him, but he keeps giving you excuses and promising that his performance will improve. What can you ask Adam to help you understand what is going on?

*situation **3** suggested questions:* Adam, I am concerned. You are not meeting your job expectations. Is there something that I should know about that might give me some perspective on why this is happening?

The bottom line is that it's easy to make assumptions about why an employee is behaving in a particular manner, but the reality is that you could be way off target in your assumption and end up losing a good employee. Be careful, especially if an employee is sending you signals that she doesn't care. Don't rush off and consult HR or your boss about her dismissal. You should first take some time to clarify the situation and make sure you perceive the situation the same way the employee does. Your goal is to understand why the behavior is taking place and not to make assumptions.

Even with good performers, it can be important to ask clarifying questions and get the employee's point of view. You don't want to come across as if you're arbitrarily raising the bar. Instead, you want to lead the employee to raise the bar on her own.

Sample Script   *"We need to talk"*

RYAN: Have you had a chance to look at your performance review?

MAX: Yes, it stinks! I can't believe you rated me a three. I expected a four at least, maybe even a five!

RYAN: Tell me more. Why did you think that you should be rated a four or five?

MAX: Because I accomplished all of my key results! I work harder than anyone else. Other people don't contribute nearly what I do.

RYAN: So you think that accomplishing your key results should give you a rating of a four or five. Do I understand your view correctly?

MAX: Yes, that and how hard I work.

RYAN: I understand that you see yourself as a hard worker. I would agree. The problem is that last year we agreed that you would work on improving your ability to work well with others and to work more collaboratively. Unfortunately, I have not seen these areas improve. So, I rated you down on those things.

MAX: That's just bullshit! The rest of the team never gives me a break. They're just out to show me up. They don't ever include me in the loop.

RYAN: So you would like the team to include you in their discussions?

MAX: Damn straight!

RYAN: Well, what I would like is for you to make a list of all the ways that the team could include you more. Please be specific and we will sit down with them and come up with a plan.

MAX: Okay.

RYAN: What other ideas do you have for improving in these areas where we've still marked a need for you to improve?

MAX: I don't know.

RYAN: Well, you could take a class to improve your conflict and communication skills.

MAX: Oh, yeah sure, charm school.

RYAN: Well, we have to come up with something.

MAX: They know how I am, they just won't accept me.

RYAN: Well, the problem is, I've observed some of this behavior also so we need to find a way to overcome these areas. Let's set up a follow-up meeting. I'll come up with my own list and perhaps you can think of some more ideas before then.

RYAN: Okay.

Employee Conversation Don'ts	Employee Conversation Dos
Delay performance reviews.	*Do performance reviews on time.*
Dance around the issue.	*Tell the truth.*
Be vague.	*Be specific.*
Only talk about performance once a year.	*Manage performance all year.*
Just tell the employee what you think.	*Ask the employee what they think.*

"We need to talk"

Chapter 4

How to Talk to Lazy, Gossiping, or Sloppy Workers

NATE THOMSON STOOD outside the data entry center and sighed. No one had yet noticed that the boss was at the door so, of course, very little work was getting accomplished. Samantha filed her nails as if her life depended on the perfect point; Kathy and Sam had their heads together, giggling and laughing; and Tom just stared out the window. No one seemed to understand that the purpose of work was well, work.

He knew he needed to talk to them . . . but had no idea what to say.

The Ideal

You know all those management and leadership books about vision and praise? That's what we're talking about here. Ideally, you would create an environment so uplifting in terms of your vision and role models who "walk the talk" that people would just want to do what you asked, would be self-motivated, and would require very little correction.

> *"We need to talk"*
>
> Negative reinforcement—punishment of some sort—does work in the short run with both rats and people, but in the long run it creates bad habits and backlash.

Ideally, you would praise the good and ignore the bad. Years ago, psychologist B. F. Skinner trained a lot of rats to show that the most effective techniques are actually this positive kind of reward system in which you reward the actions you want and ignore the rest. He called this "positive reinforcement."

One of the most entertaining ways to learn about this technique is to read Amy Sutherland's book *Kicked, Bitten and Scratched: Life Lessons at the World's Premier School for Exotic Animal Trainers.* Ms. Sutherland spent a year studying with animal trainers who work with wild animals in zoos and shows. She then wrote a popular piece for the *New York Times* explaining how she tried the magic techniques on her husband.

What's the secret? The technique is brilliant in its simplicity, although difficult in the discipline required to execute the plan. You reward the behavior you like and ignore the behavior you don't like. Sutherland—like most of us with our significant others—had been using the exact opposite technique: nagging. Once she switched to appreciating her husband for doing things she liked, and ignoring what she loathed, his behavior changed.

Sutherland used what wild-animal trainers call "approximations," rewarding the small steps toward learning a completely new behavior. Just as animals don't learn to balance balls in one session,

Sutherland found that husbands don't pick up dirty socks with one reminder.

Say, for example, that you want the slacker in your group to start doing something—anything!—that looks like working instead of surfing porn sites all day. If he turns in one project—even if three more remain outstanding—you would not grouse, but instead applaud and offer him a reward (such as candy). You get the idea. Acknowledge any movement toward success, no matter how small, and ignore the rest.

Simple gratitude can be useful in building bonds with your employees and getting them to do what you want. Believe it or not, several studies have shown that people who feel gratitude toward particular individuals (even when they never directly express it) experience closer and higher-quality relationships with them. As the world's most prominent researcher and writer about gratitude, Robert Emmons, notes, when you become truly aware of the value of someone, you are likely to treat them better, perhaps producing an "upward spiral," a sort of positive feedback loop in which strong relationships give you something to be grateful for, and in turn, fortify those very same relationships. In addition, a grateful person is a more positive person, and the research reveals that positive people are better liked by others and more likely to have people cooperate with them.

Furthermore, it will be easier for you to exercise the control you as a boss need in order to reward people effectively if you have already created a connection with them, that invisible glue that holds relationships together. As writer Daniel Goleman writes in *Social Intelligence*, we're literally wired for connection at the level of our brain chemistry. We resonate with the emotions of others.

And as psychiatrist and author Edward Hollowell has observed, monkeys and small children die from lack of social contact. Literally, we connect or we die.

Why am I harping on the benefits of connection? Because although animal-training techniques may be extremely effective, applying them to the creatures in your particular workplace zoo may challenge your endurance. In order to stay focused, you may need to focus on the rewards to you of creating more intimacy in your life.

Values and Conflicts

When using her knowledge about reinforcement with her husband, Sutherland also tracked her husband as one would an exotic animal. What are its habits? Diet? Likes? Dislikes? Does it sleep in trees or under benches? You might try the same with the employee who's exhibiting annoying behaviors. Knowledge is power, and makes training easier.

Frequently, manager/employee conflicts occur because the manager and employee have very different values. It's difficult to manage people if you don't know what they value. Learn what your difficult employees value, and you will know how to reward them.

In finding out what your employees value, try to stay away from value judgments—just because they like going out dancing or horse racing doesn't mean you have to strap on your salsa shoes or head to the track. Just take that information and put it to good use.

It's amazing that leaders try to inspire people without knowing what they value. How can you inspire anyone if you don't know what motivates them?

One of the strangest values conflicts I've ever mediated involved a manager, June, and Sally, the assistant to the CEO, both working for a large nonprofit. The manager and the assistant did not get along, and their feud had escalated to the point that they weren't speaking to one another. The CEO, a classic conflict-avoider, asked me to mediate the dispute.

One of June's employees had a standing appointment to have her nails done every Thursday in the middle of the day. Because this employee was an excellent worker, June let her take the time off. Sally thought that it was wrong to take time off in the middle of the day for such a frivolous endeavor. June countered that was a value judgment and basically, none of Sally's business; she just had different values.

The problem with the "great nail standoff" was the CEO hadn't clarified his own ideas about the flexible work schedule that he'd reluctantly agreed to implement. Should employees be allowed to leave for any reason, or should it be limited to manager-approved absences?

June thought that giving her employee time off in the middle of the day was an important motivator for her employee and insisted that allowing her this time paid off in the long run. Sally had different values; the CEO just didn't want to be involved at all.

My own assessment was that June was a smart manager who had gone to the trouble to find out what her employees valued and to reward them with things that they wanted—whether or not she agreed with their choices. As long as they completed their work, she didn't care.

Seek out evidence of what your slacker employees value. Do they wake up for certain activities but sleep through others? Do you notice them talking animatedly in the lunchroom on some topics? Study their habits and gather clues as to what useful rewards might be.

Another technique is, of course, the obvious one: You could just ask. Some questions to help you discover values might include the following:

- I've been noticing that you don't seem as interested in your job as you used to be. What company reward might be a good motivator for you?
- I'm curious about your other jobs. Were there any where you felt consistently motivated? What kinds of rewards or incentives were offered?
- What's your dream job? What do you think would motivate you to do your best in that field?

Talking with Slackers

If you loathe managing slackers, you're in good company. In a recent study by Leadership IQ, a training and research organization based in Washington, D.C., 87 percent of employees reported that working besides low-performing colleagues had made them want to change jobs. Further, 93 percent also claimed that working with low performers decreased their productivity.

"Low performers can feel like emotional vampires, sucking the energy out of everyone around them," says Leadership IQ chief executive Mark Murphy, whose company surveyed 70,305 employees, managers, and executives from 116 companies and organizations. Those surveyed were asked to list characteristics of a low performer. The top five characteristics were

1. A negative attitude;
2. A tendency to stir up trouble;
3. A tendency to blame others;

4. A lack of initiative; and
5. Incompetence.

Low performers excel in the art of work avoidance. They spend more time arguing their way out of tasks than it would take to simply complete them. They are good at identifying problems but not so good at finding solutions. They have well-crafted excuses for not getting anything done. And their sloth is often at the expense of more conscientious coworkers, who must pick up their slack.

Ironically, many slackers do not see themselves as slackers, preferring instead to blame others. Of the 87 percent of employees who want to get away from low performers, half are probably low performers themselves, if research can be believed. For instance, more than half of American workers are not engaged in their jobs, according to a recent survey by Gallup. Most are "sleepwalking though their workdays," Gallup says. But 19 percent are what Gallup calls the "actively disengaged." The 23 million "actively disengaged" U.S. workers cost the national economy more than 300 billion a year in lost productivity.

Shaking up the Slackers

In short, if companies hope to keep their best employees, they should dump their worst. Otherwise, low performers will start dictating the company's cultures: Productivity, quality, and service will all decline precipitously, and high performers will avoid your organization like the proverbial plague.

Former General Electric CEO Jack Welch famously fired the bottom 10 percent of his workforce each year. Welch used sports metaphors to justify this extreme practice, saying he wanted to work with A-team performers. He was roundly criticized as callous by some and as indiscriminate by others, who pointed out that for some jobs, there's just not that much differentiation between the lowest and highest performance. Yet GE did flourish under his management. "I think the cruelest thing you can do to somebody is give them a head fake . . . nice appraisals . . . [are] false kindness," writes Welch in the book *The Jack Welch Lexicon of Leadership.*

> **"We need to talk"**
>
> Slackers can intimidate most leaders. Many managers simply don't want to deal with them. They will duck down a side hallway just to avoid engagement.

Most managers avoid addressing the problem of slackers. When I teach management classes, for example, I routinely ask how many of them have someone on a performance improvement plan. Usually one or two of them do, despite surveys that show at least 20 percent of the employees in any workplace perform poorly.

There's plenty of false kindness and management wimpiness going around. In the Leadership IQ survey, only 14 percent of senior executives said their company effectively managed low performers. And only 17 percent of middle managers said they feel comfortable removing low performers.

Managers avoid slackers for many reasons. Some may lack the skills to manage performance effectively. Good performance management can be difficult and requires a manager to make certain that he or she knows what behavior constitutes acceptable performance and what results they seek. Many managers really do not know what the criteria should be, beyond counting face time in the office.

Other managers may be paranoid about confronting an employee who is different from them in some way; that is, of a different gender, race, or generation. Finally, many managers don't want to make anyone feel bad, or they lack confrontation and conflict skills.

Can slackers be fired for goofing off at work? Ask the hapless New York City clerk fired by Mayor Michael Bloomberg for being discovered playing a game of solitaire when Bloomberg and a group of reporters trooped into the clerk's office on a tour. Bloomberg canned him on the spot, which is legal if employees have been warned that such behavior isn't allowed.

What to do about slackers? This is the standard coach, counsel, warn, plan, and then fire. Document, document, document all along the way.

Coaching

Ideally, coaching is what you do every day. If you have an employee who spends more time making paper airplanes than working, remember the wild animal approximations. Small rewards received immediately and frequently seem to have more effect in performance than larger rewards delivered long after performances and infrequently. A $5 gift card may do more to motivate an employee than a potential promotion in the vague future. This is especially true for younger workers. Studies have shown that frequent specific feedback from managers, delivered shortly after a good performance, is all an employee needs to make good work a habit.

Conversely, when you need to correct behavior, you have to ask people to improve, check for improvement, and then verbally compliment any improvement. Otherwise, employees may wonder why they should bother if no one notices the change. It's important that the feedback be specific. Saying "Great job today," leaves your employee wondering what was so great and doesn't encourage her to do it again. Try "That report had no errors and I appreciate that you caught my mistake on page nine. Way to go!" instead.

> *"We need to talk"*
>
> This doesn't mean that you no longer need to give raises, performance reviews, and promotions. Giving regular verbal rewards to your employees simply means that you'll be writing better and better reviews for employees who are happier and more motivated.

You can rarely motivate lazy people by criticizing them. Criticism leads to discouragement and bad morale. It can lead to mutiny. Compliments followed by constructive criticism are more effective. When people receive recognition for the good things they do, they feel more motivated to be productive. When you approach a slacker, make a positive observation of something he does well, and then offer him a tip about what he could improve: "Well, you've done a really great job here. Let's try to pick up the pace and get X number more like this done before lunch." Or, "You work very quickly and efficiently, but this could be a little better."

Never forget to tell people when they're doing well. Also, get to know people. Ask them about themselves at lunch, after work. Keep it light but let them see the more human side of you. Before you leave, ask someone about his plans for the weekend. Organize an outing once in a while, and invite families to a barbecue.

Save punishment for people who actively defy you with insubordination. Make them understand what impact their lack of initiative has on the entire team. Explain the impact of their actions, such as, "When I see you staring out the window, I worry that you're not getting your report done. I need you to focus on how to do that by five o'clock."

Quantify the results of the job, not the actual activity involved so that employees will know what they're working toward.

Managing Face time

Many managers are still managing by keeping track of the time that people actually spend in the office. But in the information age, especially with younger workers, it's a good idea to consider quantifying what you really want them to accomplish and judging by results, not just time. Many studies show that younger workers want the flexibility to work remotely and be judged by results.

Surprisingly, many managers are reluctant to consider this approach. Because I'm an attorney, I'm asked to do a lot of consulting projects for law firms, many of whom are having trouble keeping their best young associates, especially women. When I suggest that they allow attorneys who have done well the privilege of working at home or other out-of-the-office locations, many older partners are horrified. *We might need them for something!*, they cry.

Never mind that most legal work these days, even in-office conferences, is conducted over the phone or the Internet. Never mind that attorneys keep track of their time in tenths of an hour, so it's very easy to quantify who is working or not working. The resistance to change remains strong in many professions.

Even if you don't decide to loosen up on where the work actually needs to be done, however, you'll benefit from setting specific, measurable objectives for the job. These need to be results that are quantifiable, that are easy to understand, and that everyone can agree on. Of course, these objectives should actually add value to the organization. Employees—especially the best and the brightest—eventually rebel against busy work. Maybe the slacker you're trying to shape up isn't lazy but rather bored or failing to see the larger meaning in what you're asking him to accomplish.

Sloppy Workers

In managing sloppy workers, you can use many of the techniques mentioned above, especially approximations and small rewards and praise.

It's important to remember that it's part of an employee's responsibility to perform her work with reasonable care. You do have the right, and indeed, the responsibility to require this. But many employees can be overwhelmed with large projects. Break things down into small bites so that they can absorb and learn. Also, make sure that they're behaviorally specific, rather than vague. Examples would include the following:

Vague	Behaviorally Specific
Don't be so sloppy!	Put each bottle into the holder when you finish.
Be more careful!	I need all letters to clients to be free from typographical and other errors.
You're messy!	When you're meeting with customers, please comb your hair and wear an ironed shirt.

Be aware also that some people really struggle with neatness. They may have large or fine motor-control problems, which interfere with the brain's ability to tell the body what to do and the body's ability to follow through on directions. Some people with dyspraxia and other problems have a disconnect between the brain and the body: The brain is telling the body what to do but the body is not getting it.

Some workers who appear to be sloppy workers may have other brain chemistry problems such as ADHD or depression. These kinds of things can cause problems with the prefrontal cortex (PFC) of the brain, which is the area of the brain that governs planning and organization. Even workers who are smart, funny, and generally good people, if they have PFC problems they will not have a good conductor for the other areas of the brain that do function well.

"We need to talk"

This is not to say that you should accept substandard work. Just keep in mind that some people may sincerely be doing the best they can to meet whatever exacting standards you may have, but they simply cannot get their brains and their bodies to cooperate.

In such cases, you may have to probe gently to find out what's really going on. Chances are they have planning and organization problems in other areas of their lives, but you don't want to go too deeply into that arena because it would create a privacy violation. You could ask a series of questions such as the following:

- Is there anything at work that I'm doing, or that anyone else is doing that's interfering with your success?
- If there's anything in your home life that's interfering with your success that's none of my business, but you may want to contact employee assistance.

Then if they do open that door, you can listen carefully and learn, but do not pry. You might also ask them to sit down with you and brainstorm what might help them meet your standards of doing neater or better work.

Also, check out your own standards. Some bosses expect higher standards than are necessary for every project. If you have an overall good worker who doesn't measure up to your standards, consider whether your standards can be adjusted on some projects so that they don't feel overwhelmed with perfectionist details.

Losing basically good employees is expensive. In addition to the standard costs of advertising and interviewing, there are training and orientation costs. Many times this can add up to 100 to 150 percent of an employee's salary. You lose productivity from other employees during interviewing, searching, training, lost clients, and so on. Right now, it's an employee's market; we have a national labor shortage. It's much better practice to try to save an employee than to start all over again, even if the process of correcting bad habits may be tedious.

Gossiping Workers

Ask employees how they feel about gossip, and you'll get the same answer from all of them: They dislike it. Yet ask those same people if gossip exists in their workplace, and you'll get the same answer: absolutely. So, what gives?

Social scientists tell us gossip is a time-honored and popular way to increase social functioning and connection. The truth is, we all gossip, because we all talk about other people. When we say we don't like gossip, what we really mean is that we don't like gossip about us or people we like.

The problem in the workplace, of course, is that gossip can poison environments, reduce productivity, and perpetuate nasty rumors. The best leaders make it clear that they will simply not tolerate gossip in any form. That means, of course, that they have to "walk the talk" and not gossip themselves.

The best way to deal with gossip is to head it off at the pass by making sure that your employees know from the start that you will not tolerate gossip. If you do that, and if you lead by example, you'll be much less likely to invite them to engage in this bothersome activity.

When you talk about gossip with employees initially, it's best to do so in a group and to give specific examples of why gossip is most damaging: company rumors, unfounded speculation about coworkers' personal lives, unannounced promotions, or whatever makes your personal list.

After that, you need to up the ante by making sure that employees understand that beyond gossip lies defamation. *Defamation* is a legal term that means saying something false about another person that interferes with his or her reputation. The courts take defamation very seriously, especially in a workplace setting, because they realize that no matter what our job title, the only thing we really have to sell is our reputation. Once our reputation is damaged, we have nothing left to give at work.

As a manager, you have a special obligation to watch what your employees are saying after there's been a complaint or an investigation of some act of discrimination, threats, or other misconduct. The rumor mill goes into overdrive after one of these incidents. Unfortunately, most of the rumors are untrue (in fact, much worse than the truth) and can lead to defamation claims.

"We need to talk"

It helps to ask your troops to imagine how they would feel if someone were spreading rumors about them. Personnel matters need to be kept private, as your employees would agree if they were going through a complaint or an investigation.

If you've had one of these upsets in your workgroup, you need to call a meeting, warn them about defamation issues, and make sure that they understand that you will impose discipline for anyone you hear has talked about this issue. You may be able to convince HR or legal to come in and provide a sanitized version of what did actually occur so that employees don't have to keep speculating. Regardless, it is your job to squash any rumors.

Sample Script

"We need to talk"

RYAN: I've called you in here because I've noticed something that concerns me.

KATHY: Oh really, what?

RYAN: I was looking into the data entry center the other day and noticed that you and Dave were laughing and whispering. I'm wondering if you've thought about how that might make others feel.

KATHY: Well, no, I didn't realize that anyone noticed.

RYAN: I've also heard that there are rumors being spread about the recent investigation. I'm not sure where these rumors are coming from, but I wanted to meet with people to remind them that those rumors are not tolerated in this organization. As you recall, we talked about how damaging that can be to someone's reputation in the last staff meeting and how it could lead to defamation, not to mention termination. I'm wondering what your thoughts are about this topic? Have you heard any of these rumors?

KATHY: Well, I didn't even think about that. I have heard some rumors . . .

RYAN: I just want to make it clear that everyone in the staff understands my position on this subject and that no one contributes to these rumors.

KATHY: I'm sorry. I guess we just didn't think.

Employee Conversation Don'ts	Employee Conversation Dos
Beat around the bush.	*Get straight to the point.*
Give vague directives.	*Use approximations to change behavior.*
Tolerate lazy or sloppy work.	*Set standards.*
Tolerate gossip.	*Challenge gossip.*
Ignore people.	*Create connections.*

"We need to talk"

Chapter 5

How to Confront Alcohol, Drugs, and Violence at Work

STEVE SNIDER WALKED down the hall, dragging his feet and wishing he could be somewhere else. Ed was a brilliant associate, but he'd come in late too many times lately, and he'd almost slugged a client at the last client reception. Everyone in the office drank—it seemed to come with the territory of trial attorneys—but Ed's had gotten out of control. Steve needed to confront him today before something worse happened.

The problem was, Steve had no idea what to say.

Basic Employment Law Principles

How common are threats and violence at work? A 2000 study done by the USPS Commission on a Safe and Secure Workplace found what it called "a disturbing and unacceptable level of violence in the American workplace," with one out of every twenty employees reporting a physical assault, and one in three saying they were verbally abused on the job.

> **"We need to talk"**
>
> In 2002, homicide was the third leading cause of death on the job, topped only by motor vehicle accidents and falls. More than 1.8 million workdays and $55 million in wages are lost every year due to workplace violence, according to the Bureau of Justice Statistics.

Although no one can predict where and when violence will erupt at a job site, employers can be held liable for the resulting injuries. When an employee gets violent or abusive, it's the manager's duty to remain calm and try to defuse the situation, according to a 2001 federal appellate case involving a situation in which an employee mocked, used racial slurs against, and then head-butted his boss. The boss slapped the employee away and cursed back at him. Was that okay? No, said the court, and the employer was well within its rights when it demoted the boss to a nonsupervisory position. More importantly, violence can be reduced—and even prevented—through some commonsense precautions. One thing you can do to prevent violence is establish and enforce a clear policy against violence—as well as provide employees with proper training.

Establishing and Enforcing an Anti-Violence Policy

You and your employees have a right to be safe at work. If someone's threatening physical harm or engaging in physical abuse at work, he's violating the law as well as, most likely, your organization's policy.

Most organizations have strong policies these days about threats and violence. If your organization does not, you should talk to HR or your boss about establishing one. Here's a typical example:

* * *

Every employee has a strong interest and responsibility in helping to maintain a safe working environment for themselves and their coworkers. The company strives to ensure a safe environment for all employees, and this policy is issued and administered to support this commitment.

The company and its employees will have zero tolerance for threats and violent acts in the workplace. Examples of this could include intimidating, threatening, or hostile behaviors such as physical abuse, vandalism, arson, sabotage, use of weapons, carrying weapons onto company property, or any other act that, in management's opinion, is inappropriate to the workplace. Employees who observe or have knowledge of any violation of this policy should immediately report it to company management, human resources, or corporate security, and should directly contact proper law enforcement authorities if there is an immediate serious threat to the safety or health of themselves or others.

* * *

As a manager, you should be enforcing your organization's policies. If you see more than one of the warning signs of violence listed below, you need to confront the person, or, if she is a security risk, call security, legal, and HR immediately.

The good news is that every case of workplace violence has been studied thoroughly. The vast majority of perpetrators have been with their organizations for years. Usually they felt that they had been denied a promotion they thought they were entitled to, or they had been terminated unjustly. In virtually every case, the perpetrators made threats beforehand.

Most people point to the post office as an example of a workplace that is prone to violence, but in reality there's no higher percentage of threats and violence in the post office than there is in most other workplaces. The difference is the number of people working there: There are actually more people employed at the post office than any other place in the United States, except the military. So we have the perception that there's more violence, but the reality is that the post office is just average in this respect.

Warning Signs of Violence

Here are the warning signs of violence. Most people who erupt into violence will exhibit more than one of these characteristic behaviors:

- Makes direct and indirect threats
- Mood swings, depression, bizarre statements, delusions of persecution
- History of violence
    - Domestic violence, verbal abuse, antisocial activities

- Romantic obsession
  - Physical or romantic obsession
- Substance abuse
  - Trouble with alcohol or drug addiction
- Depressive behavior
  - Self-destructive behavior
  - Loner behavior or isolation
  - Unkempt physical appearance, despair, sluggish decision-making
- Pathological blamer
  - Accepts no responsibility for his or her actions
  - Constantly blames coworkers, employer, government, "the system"
- Impaired ability to function
  - Poor impulse control
- Obsession with weapons
  - Ownership of gun or gun collection, combined with antisocial behavior
  - Fascination with shooting skills or weapon-related activity
- Personality disorder
  - Antisocial or borderline personality disorders
  - Irritable, aggressive, often involved in disputes or fights with others
  - Steals or destroys property with little remorse
  - Borderline personality; shows moodiness, instability, impulsive action, easily agitated

Clearly, you have both the right and the responsibility to intervene if you see behavior that is threatening or violent or that you believe might lead to threats and violence. This is an area where being proactive is always a good idea. Don't wait until it's too late.

While actual incidents of violence may be rare, the consequences are so grave that you must take action ahead of the curve.

Preventing Violence

Experts agree that effective pre-employment background checks are crucial. Before hiring any applicant, check references and ask specifically if there is any history of violent or harassing behavior. Even if the references refuse to answer the question, you have taken reasonable steps to screen out potentially violent employees, and that will help you if you're ever sued.

Once you've hired employees, you have an obligation to provide a safe workplace. You want to create a violence-free environment. Here are some suggestions, based on a recent report from the International Association of Chiefs of Police:

- Take advantage of community resources.
  - ➤ Use law enforcement and security experts to provide crime prevention information, perform building security inspections, and teach employees how to avoid becoming victims.
- Enforce security procedures.
  - ➤ Make sure employees know and honor policies about badges, identification, and keys.
  - ➤ Limit outsider access to areas beyond the lobby/reception area.
  - ➤ Establish an international emergency code word or phone number.
  - ➤ Get employee input on security weak spots (bad lighting in parking lot, etc.).
  - ➤ Encourage employees who are victims of domestic violence to provide security a picture of the batterer and a copy of any court order of protection.

- Establish ground rules for behavior.
  - ➤ Inform employees about policies against inappropriate behavior, violent acts, and possession of weapons and drugs on company premises.
  - ➤ Enforce policies through consistent discipline; that is, written warning or termination of every threat-maker when the complaint is substantiated.
  - ➤ Encourage employees to report threats, harassment, and other aggressive behavior.
  - ➤ Respect privacy and confidentiality rights of all employees during any investigation.
  - ➤ Make it easy for employees to raise suggestions about reducing risks and improving working conditions.
  - ➤ Remind employees that employee assistance programs are available to help with emotional, marital, financial, and substance abuse problems.
  - ➤ Conduct exit interviews when employees retire, quit, or are terminated to identify violence-related security or management problems. In those interviews, don't just ask "Why are you leaving," but "What was happening at work when you first started thinking about leaving?"

While pleading self-defense in court might absolve an employee from criminal liability for violent acts, in most states an employer is justified in firing or disciplining a worker who behaves violently in violation of company policy. As a California appellate court noted in a 2003 decision upholding the termination of an employee who fought back against a coworker: "[A]n employer which gave its employees the option to choose 'fight' over 'flight' when confronted with workplace violence, might itself be violating public policy."

If you are ever threatened or put into a potentially violent situation, there are a number of things you can do to calm things down:

- Project calmness. Move and speak slowly, quietly, and confidently. Try to listen actively and empathetically.
- Encourage the person to talk and listen patiently to what they say. Let him know that you are interested in what's being said. Try to acknowledge, by repeating back to him, the person's feelings. Indicate that you can see that he is upset and must be in pain.
- Sit or stand in a relaxed yet attentive posture. You should try to position yourself at a right angle rather than directly in front of the other person.
- Do not let an angry employee block your access to an exit.
- Ask for small, specific favors, such as asking the person to move to a quieter area. This can help you think and help the employee see you as a person with whom he can cooperate to solve her problems.
- Try to establish ground rules if threatening behavior persists. Describe what will happen if the employee engages in any violent behavior.
- Use delaying tactics that will give the person time to calm down. Offer him a drink of water or coffee.
- Be reassuring and point out that the employee does have other choices. Offer to help her write a letter or make a call to the person she's upset with. Break big problems into smaller, more manageable problems.
- If the employee criticizes you, try not to get defensive. Accept whatever feedback she gives you. If there could be some truth to a complaint, use statements such as "You might be right" or "I shouldn't have done that." If the criticism seems totally false, ask clarifying questions to get her to give you more information.

- While you're talking with the employee, respect his personal space. Don't make any sudden movement or invade his boundaries.
- Do not appear to be apathetic, brush off the employee's concerns, or use coldness or condescension, such as "well those are the rules," or give her the run-around. Do not reject all her demands from the start. Instead, keep asking for more information, use clarifying questions, and keep her talking.
- Be careful about how you stand. If you pose in challenging stances, such as directly opposite someone, hands on your hips, or crossing your arms, you could appear threatening to an already emotional person. You should avoid any physical contact, finger pointing, or staring contests.
- Be careful not to make any sudden movements, which can be seen as threatening. Pay attention to the tone, volume, and rate of your speech.
- Don't try to challenge, threaten, or dare the individual. Don't belittle him or make him feel foolish.
- Finally, call security or dial 911 as soon as possible.

Alcohol and Drugs at Work

Most workplaces have policies against alcohol and drugs at work, and you have every right to enforce those, as you should. You move into gray areas when employees have drinks after work or when someone appears to be under the influence of alcohol or drugs on the job.

After-Work Drinking

Many workplaces have social situations that encourage drinking. Silicon Valley companies host Friday afternoon beer busts. Law firms may have bars or sherry sipping. At a construction site, the boss and his workers may hit the local bar or even hang around the lot drinking after hours. Sales departments may be expected to wine and dine clients.

Many employers think that this drinking benefits the bottom line by encouraging informal networking. The problem is that you can create legal liability. If the company provides free drinks and drunken employees hurt themselves, they can claim workers' compensation. Because the drinks were free, the courts have found that the employees did not voluntarily become intoxicated.

On the other hand, if a company party is completely voluntary and the employer charges for drinks, the company isn't liable for workers' compensation when employees hurt themselves.

Free booze or not, if a drunk employee injures another employee, that person can claim benefits from the company. If the drunken employee drives away from the party and kills or injures a third party, the company may be held liable the same as any other social host or a restaurant bartender.

As manager, your job is to keep employees safe and prevent accidents. Be careful not to push alcohol on others. Serve as a good role model by monitoring your own and your employees' drinking. If employees seem visibly intoxicated, you shouldn't allow them to work or drive. Call a cab if you have to.

When Employees Appear to Be under the Influence at Work

First, be very careful about making judgments about the causes of anyone's incapacity at work. Many other kinds of medical conditions, such as epilepsy or diabetes, can mimic alcohol or drug problems. Your job as a manager is to focus on performance. If you see performance problems that you suspect are due to alcohol or drug abuse, instruct the worker what proper performance looks like using the specifics that we've covered in previous chapters. You have to be very cautious about accusing anyone of being under the influence of drugs and alcohol because doing so could be considered a violation of privacy.

"We need to talk"

State laws vary widely on this issue. The Idaho Supreme Court held in 1991 that a company was liable for the death of a pedestrian killed by an employee who drank too much at an office party. Another man drank on a business trip, passed out drunk in the snow, and had to have his fingers amputated because of frostbite. Remarkably, the Wisconsin Supreme Court, in a 2001 decision, found that he was entitled to workers' compensation.

Workers have a right to keep their private life private. Drug and alcohol problems that are serious enough to require medical attention may lead to a leave request or a disability claim, as covered in Chapter 6, but that is a separate issue.

When you see someone behaving in a way that leads you to suspect alcohol or drug use, figure out how it interferes with individual or team performance. If it doesn't interfere with individual or team performance, *stop*! Why are you addressing this? You need to have a business reason to do so.

When you do decide to intervene, here are some examples of appropriate things to say:

Employee Conversation Don'ts	Employee Conversation Dos
You're drinking too much.	*You came in late five times this month and at the client dinner you slurred your words.*
You were drunk at the party.	*You took off your clothes and danced on the table.*
You're stoned.	*You fell asleep at your machine.*

As usual, you need to document, document, document the specific behavior and performance problem. You then need to use 1-2-3-Go! to request different behavior. If the behavior doesn't improve, put the employee on a performance plan, and terminate them if they don't shape up.

Drug Testing

Many employers want to have mandatory or random drug testing in order to keep problem employees away from their workplace, but this is a technical area that requires real knowledge.

There are six types of drug tests: pre-employment tests to screen out applicants, "for cause"-testing of employees upon reasonable suspicion of intoxication, postaccident tests, regularly scheduled tests (usually part of a general, required physical), unannounced random tests, and follow-up tests to confirm an employee is maintaining sobriety after testing positive.

"We need to talk"

All this doesn't mean that you can't be compassionate if someone is unfortunate enough to be mired in drug and alcohol problems. You can certainly say some version of this:

"If there's anything going on at work that's affecting your performance, please let me know. If there's anything that's going on in your personal life that's affecting your performance, that's none of my business, but we do have employee assistance so you may want to contact them."

And then, of course, if the employee does come up with some specific information about drug or alcohol issues, you can be empathetic and deal with that. You want to open that door but not walk through it. Unless you're a trained medical professional, therapist, or recovering alcoholic or addict yourself, you want to avoid giving advice in this area. Stay compassionate but focus on performance and enforce the specific boundaries and performance standards that your workplace requires. It can be very tempting to want to rescue someone in this situation, but you won't be doing any good by trying to handle it yourself.

In one study, 69 percent of private-sector companies were found to conduct drug tests, yet only 5 percent of workers came up positive. Even when employers reasonably suspected drug abuse, less than 15 percent of employees tested positive.

This has led many advocates to claim that drug testing is an invasion of privacy and overly broad. They make this argument based on the theory that drug testing invades our bodies, a very personal zone for most of us. Unfortunately, a urinalysis not only reveals illegal drug use, but also any other medication taken for depression, HIV, epilepsy, high blood pressure, and other private and sensitive medical conditions. It is basically surveillance of someone's private life.

Because of these concerns, the U.S. Supreme Court has found that employers must have a *compelling* reason to test for drugs. Compelling reasons have included safety issues, such as upholding the right to test employees for drugs immediately after work-related accidents. The Supreme Court has limited the availability of drug testing for employees currently working because it is overly broad and results in a lot of false positives—up to 1 to 2 percent. That may sound like a small amount, but given that 10 million employees are tested each year, hundreds of thousands are being falsely accused of drug use based on faulty tests. Some experts believe the rate of false positives is as high as 62 percent.

Despite these problems, the Supreme Court has upheld drug testing for jobs where there are health and safety concerns such as employees with national security clearances, airline personnel, corrections officers, transportation employees, chemical weapons plant employees, Army civilian employees, police officers, nuclear power plant workers, and water treatment plant workers.

What about testing for drugs when you believe that you have a reasonable suspicion that employees are using on the job? A 1997 California appellate case provides a cautionary tale. A senior manager saw an executive secretary sitting with her elbows on her knees, looking down at the ground. She didn't move or answer when he asked her what was wrong. He called HR and told them he thought she was having "female problems."

"We need to talk"

In addition to federal cases, there's been a lot of state-level litigation about drug testing. Every state has some privacy protections, and fifteen states have statutes specifically regulating drug tests. In most states, pre-employment testing has been upheld, but not random tests for employees in nonsensitive positions.

The HR director came by and observed that the secretary's "speech was slurred, that her demeanor was lethargic, that she was swaying, that her eye contact was not there, that she seemed to be deliberate in her answers, she was very controlled and very deliberate." Based on these observations, the secretary was ordered to take a drug test, and when she refused, she was fired.

When she sued, both the manager and the HR director admitted on the stand that they had no training in detecting drug abuse. Amazingly, the company allowed the secretary to drive herself to testing and then was allowed to drive herself home—a distance of over sixty miles! The court pointed that these facts indicated that management didn't believe that she was really impaired.

Because the whole area of drug testing is such a moving target, you should seek competent legal counsel about the law and the practice in your community and industry before you begin such a program.

Alternatives to Traditional Drug Testing

There are other, less invasive alternatives to drug testing. Performance Factors, for example, has developed tests that measure people's reaction time, visual acuity, and other job-related abilities. Such a test doesn't invade the person's body or privacy. It measures when people are actually impaired, before they have accidents, and it catches performance programs due to sleep deprivation, depression, or hangovers.

Much like a video game, the test is used by companies in the steel and transportation industries to test employees at the beginning of each workday.

The Bottom Line on Alcohol and Drugs

What's the bottom line about your power if you think employees are using drugs or alcohol in your workplace? First, use objective, verifiable facts to prove that their work is affected. Document that they are arriving late, falling asleep, harassing other employees, or slurring their words. Document mood swings and aggressive or emotional outbursts. Start counseling and disciplining them just as you would any other underperformers.

Even if you have a legal drug-testing program, you must still document poor performance in order to justify your reasonable suspicion that an employee should take a test.

One manager failed to do this. He fired an employee for documented poor performance but, unfortunately, before he fired him, the manager said: "Off the record, I think you're a drug addict." If you're a manager, you're always *on the* record! The employee could claim defamation, violation of privacy, or infliction of emotional distress. Don't get caught in this kind of situation.

Sample Script

"We need to talk"

STEVE: Ed, I need to talk with you about last night.

ED: I know, I know, I shouldn't have snapped at Larry.

STEVE: Ed, it was more than snapping, you practically swung at him, he reared back and looked frightened. (Describes behavior, not conclusion.)

ED: Well, he's a jerk!

STEVE: He's a client. And besides that, it was a function in our office and you need to behave with dignity and decorum. You need to stop doing that. (Tells what behavior should be.) Also, you've been coming into the office at noon. Even though we don't punch clocks around here, you have to be in most mornings. Clients expect it, and partners have been looking for you.

ED: Sorry, I've just been really tired. I work better at night.

STEVE: Look, I'm worried about you. If there's anything going on here at work that's affecting your performance, please let me know. If there's anything that's going on at home that's affecting your work, that's none of my business but we do have employee assistance. (Asks appropriate questions.)

ED: Yeah, I know. I've been thinking about contacting them. The truth is all the stress has been getting to me and I know I've been drinking too much.

STEVE: Well, they can help. We value your work and want you to be a success here but you have to change your behavior.

ED: I understand.

Employee Conversation Don'ts	Employee Conversation Dos
Comment on drinking or drug use.	*Focus on performance and behavior.*
Ignore threats.	*Assess threats and enforce your policy.*
Drug-test without advice.	*Get expert advice.*

Chapter 6

How to Discuss Leave Requests, FMLA, and Disabilities with Confidence

RORY STUART STARED at one of her assistants and shook her head in disbelief. The woman had to be six months pregnant, if she were a day, but Susan hadn't said a word about it to Rory. Did she think that Rory was blind? Rory marched back into her office and slammed the door. She *must* talk with her today and find out what her plans were. The problem was she had no idea what to say.

The Leave-Request Minefield

The truth is, leave requests, disabilities, and the Family and Medical Leave Act (FMLA)—present a dangerous minefield for the uninformed—as do caregiving responsibilities. It's easy to step on the bombs spread about like traps for the unwary. While this chapter will give you a general outline of the law, your rights as a manager, and where you should slow down, in most cases you're going to need to consult your HR expert or an attorney before you respond. With the overview of this chapter, however, you'll be able to ask the right questions and get the answers you need.

Be aware, however, that some federal laws on these issues do not apply if you work for an employer with less than fifteen (in some cases) or fifty (in other situations) employees. Also, government employees are frequently subject to different rules and union contracts may provide additional wrinkles. Finally, there may be state laws that provide greater or lesser rights for employees. What is offered below is meant to be a general educational overview of the problem. As always, you need to research the laws and policies that govern your particular state and employer and you may need to consult HR or an attorney.

General Principles

While there are differences in the various leave requests, you need to follow some general principles with all of them. First, learn as much as you can about your organizations' policies, benefits, and procedures before you have your first leave conversation. Second, when you're hit with a leave request for any reason, don't respond in the moment. Listen, ask lots of open-ended but appropriate questions, and tell the employee that you'll get back to her. Then, call an expert, unless you're 100 percent sure that you know the correct answer to the request.

Basic Legal Overview

While these areas of the law are enormously complex, this section will give you an overview of the law.

Family and Medical Leave Act (FMLA)

This law has created all kinds of headaches for employers. Basically, employees have a right to twelve weeks a year of unpaid leave after their first year of employment to take care of a serious health condition for themselves or an immediately family member. Denying this leave is illegal under FMLA. The headaches come because employees do not have to take it all at once, but can do it in increments, as long as the total is no more than twelve weeks per year. You could, for example, take one day a week off for up to twelve weeks, if necessary, to take your mother to dialysis.

The FMLA was recently amended through the National Defense Authorization Act to provide up to twenty-six weeks of unpaid leave for a spouse, son, daughter, parent, or next of kin to care for a member of the armed forces or reserves who is undergoing medical treatment, recuperation, therapy, is on outpatient status, or on temporary disability for a serious injury or illness.

Disability

Most temporary disabilities will fall under the FMLA or an employer's sick leave policies. If an employee has more permanent disabilities, however, it's likely that they'll come under the federal Americans with Disabilities Act (ADA).

You cannot refuse to hire, discipline, fail to promote, or terminate someone because of a disability if it can be shown that you can reasonably accommodate the employee without undue hardship.

Accommodations may include a special screen for the employee's computer, a special chair because of back problems, or a flexible schedule to accommodate doctor's appointments. Time off may also be appropriate. A disability is defined as a "permanent and substantial impairment of a major life function." Generally, a major life function includes things such as eating, sleeping, walking, or dressing oneself. Could sex qualify as a major life function, meaning that you would be disabled if you couldn't have sex? Believe it or not, the U.S. Supreme Court had to consider just such a case in order to decide if sex was indeed a "major life function."

A truck driver hurt his back. He could still drive a truck so he couldn't claim that as a permanent impairment of a major life function: He claimed instead that the back injury affected his sex life. He argued that before he hurt his back he was able to have sex thirty or forty times a month but after the injury, he could only have sex three to four times per month. The court said that it did not believe that sex was a "major life function" such that he was disabled. They also pointed out that he had introduced no evidence of being able to have sex so often!

Mental health issues should be treated the same as physical health issues if an individual has what's known as a "biologically based illness" but currently, state and federal laws create a tangle about this one. Check your policies and with HR or an employment attorney.

How Is Reasonable Accommodation Requested?

In general, you should wait for the employee (or, in the case of an extreme psychiatric illness, a family member of the employee) to request accommodation instead of suggesting accommodation yourself. If you suggest it, you might be obligating the organization to do something that they would not be otherwise obligated to do. In addition, the ADA did away with the old system that "employers know best" and assumes that people with disabilities know what accommodations they need to be successful.

> ## "We need to talk"
>
> The ADA doesn't require mind reading, or magic words; however you should assume that an employee is requesting accommodation if he makes any statement that he needs a job modification because of a medical condition that might be a disability.

When an employee has been on extended leave for a medical problem and returns to work, sometimes he may have difficulty meeting job standards. At that time, he may qualify as disabled and need reasonable accommodation. Before you discipline, terminate, or put him on a performance plan, you should contact HR or your employment attorney, who may suggest some reasonable accommodations. If you know about an accommodation need but an employee doesn't ask, you can't ignore what you know. You should do what you can to help. In my experience, most employers, as a matter of their own policies and values, try to do this anyway, but the law has made this mandate clear.

Employer's Duty

Once an employee has requested accommodation, you have an obligation to engage with the employee in what's called an "interactive process" to determine the appropriate accommodation under the circumstances. Just because an employee requests something doesn't mean that it's automatically reasonable. You have to analyze the worker's needs. In one case, for example, an employer agreed to a request for a modified workstation because of a worker's carpal tunnel syndrome, but that accommodation wasn't effective and therefore, not "reasonable." If something doesn't work, it's not by definition reasonable.

Your employee, however, can't require you to provide a particular accommodation if something else *would* work. If the problem continues and worsens, they can also request additional accommodation as long as their requests are "reasonable."

When an employee's job changes, or she's transferred or promoted, you need to keep evaluating her needs. If the initial accommodation is no longer effective, the "interactive process" needs to start again.

One employer, for example, refused an additional accommodation to an employee whose multiple sclerosis had worsened. They fired her, and she sued and won $2,300,000.

Undue Hardship

You only need to accommodate requests that are *reasonable*. What is considered reasonable is a question of the facts and circumstances of any particular case. You don't need to accommodate any disability if it would be an *undue hardship*. Is spending a lot of money an undue hardship? As one employment lawyer observed: "As far as the government is concerned, spending money is never an undue hardship!"

In most cases, buying equipment is found to be reasonable. If the accommodation would "fundamentally alter the nature of the business" by creating a significant difficulty or expense for the whole company, not just your group, you may be able to argue it's an undue hardship.

When the ADA passed, Congress recognized that hiring and keeping people with disabilities would cost more and made the decision to shift the cost from social security and other sources, to the employers. When the ADA was being considered, business lobbyists asked Congress to place a $15,000 cap on the amount an employer would be required to spend for any particular disability. This request was defeated, leading the courts to assume that an employer could be required to spend more.

According to a report from the Office of Vocational Rehabilitations (OVR), however, most fears of expensive accommodation remain unfounded. Over half of the people with disabilities were accommodated at no extra costs, while another 30 percent required expenditures of less than $500.

You'd be wise to do your part to retain a disabled employee. The OVR report found 91 percent of disabled workers had an average or better productivity on the job than other employees. 75 percent had better safety records, and able-bodied workers' turnover rate was 11:1 compared to people with disabilities. After accommodation, 55 percent of the people with disabilities had better attendance than able-bodied workers, and only 5 percent had worse records. Remind yourself of these stellar statistics if you or your upper management is resistant to allowing accommodations.

When Does an Extended Leave Become Unreasonable?

You may wonder what to do if you have an employee with a disability who needs more than the twelve weeks of leave provided by the FMLA. How much time off can he take before you can argue that it's an undue hardship and terminate him? First, you must consider these questions:

- Can you find temporary help available?
- Are the job functions essential?
- Will work delays impact the company?

- Exactly how much time off is requested?
- Is the person in question a good employee?

You've hired someone because you need her to work, and the courts agree that regular and reliable attendance is an essential function of a job. Yet the courts also stress that you have to be fair, especially with a long-term employee. Still, requests for indefinite leave have been rejected as unreasonable, since the purpose of the ADA is to allow disabled people to work, not to hold a job forever.

Check your own company policy. Courts will look to it to determine what is reasonable. In one case, for example, two short leaves (two to four weeks each) due to flare-ups of lupus were found to be reasonable, particularly since the employer took six months to fill the employee's position after she was fired. In another case, a worker's request for a short extension of her one-month leave for depression was held reasonable. And, in a third case, the court found that the employer violated the ADA by rejecting a senior employee's request for six weeks paid leave because company policy provided up to thirty weeks of paid leave for such employees.

In general, the courts have required more protection and accommodation for long-term employees. This is important to remember when you talk to an employee. Be sure to take into account the length of his employment.

Telecommuting

Can telecommuting be a reasonable accommodation for a disability? The courts are split. The Equal Employment Opportunity Commission (EEOC) has said that the ADA doesn't require an employer to allow a worker to telecommute, but if an employer does offer telework to other employees, it would be discrimination to refuse such an accommodation to employees with disabilities.

> **"We need to talk"**
>
> It's important to remember that neither the FMLA nor the ADA requires you to allow an employee to slack off. Within the bounds of whatever accommodation is allowed, the employee needs to meet normal performance standards; otherwise, the employer would be discriminating against other employees.

For example, I was asked by one of my clients to investigate a claim of sex discrimination within the legal department of a high tech company. The women in the organization claimed that they were being treated differently because of sex. Specifically, they wanted to be able to work at home, especially those with small children and to have more flexible work hours.

They argued that some of the men in the department—especially one man, Bob—were granted such privileges. When I investigated, I found that Bob had erupted one night when he and another attorney were working late. He'd started shouting about suicide and throwing things. Understandably, the woman was terrified and complained to the general counsel.

Subsequently, Bob was diagnosed as having bipolar disorder, and his doctor suggested, as an accommodation under the ADA, that he work at home part of the time and cut his hours. In addition, however, his bosses started walking on eggshells around him, allowing sloppy work and not holding him to normal performance standards.

The women thought that his working at home, reduced hours, and sloppy work constituted sex discrimination. They knew nothing about the medical accommodation since such matters must be kept confidential.

After concluding my investigation, I found no discrimination based on sex, although I did inform Bob's bosses that they needed to hold him to normal performance standards for the hours he did work.

Family Responsibility Discrimination

Improperly denying someone leave, or discriminating against someone on the basis of hiring, promotions, assignments, or other benefits because of family responsibility, has led to a whole new area of the law called Family Responsibility Discrimination (FRD). A lot of this kind of discrimination is based on the perception that someone will need time off.

There's been a 400 percent increase in FRD cases in the last decade and an increase of 45 percent in pregnancy discrimination claims over the last twelve years. 92 percent of FRD cases are filed by women. Because most managers are not familiar with these issues, unlike FMLA or disabilities, here is some additional information to help keep you informed.

Essentially, FRD is discrimination based on obligations to provide care to family members. This includes pregnancy discrimination, parental discrimination, and discrimination against employees who care for sick or disabled family members.

In most cases, women claim they have been stereotyped because organizations erroneously believe that women with caregiving responsibilities lack commitment to the job and are less competent than workers without such responsibilities. The employer also often assumes that men do not need parental leave because women are still seen as primary caregivers.

Why are we seeing such an avalanche of FRD cases? Some reasons include the following:

- Half the workforce is women.
- Today, mothers of young children are twice as likely to work as their counterparts thirty years ago.
- One in four families is currently caring for an elderly family member.
- One in three families includes a disabled family member.

Interestingly, plaintiffs in FRD cases win more than 50 percent of the time, resulting in verdicts with large monetary awards, far greater than the average for other types of discrimination.

The numbers, as well as the potential lawsuits, are staggering. Support for these cases has arrived from surprising sources. In a 2003 Supreme Court case, Chief Justice Rehnquist, not known for holding liberal views on the court, voted with the majority in upholding the availability of an FMLA claim to a state employee. He emphasized that "Stereotypes about women's domestic roles are reinforced by parallel stereotypes presuming a lack of domestic responsibilities for men. . . . Those perceptions, in turn, Congress reasoned, lead to subtle discrimination that may be difficult to detect on a case-by-case basis. . . . By creating an across-the-board, routine employment benefit for all eligible employees, Congress sought to ensure that family-care leave would no longer be stigmatized as an inordinate drain on the workplace caused by female employees, and that employers could not evade leave obligations simply by hiring men."

What are some examples of sex-based discrimination of female caregivers? Examples include asking only female employees (not male employees) about child-care or caregiving responsibilities, or asking questions regarding how employees will balance travel duties or heavy workloads with child-care responsibilities.

It's also impermissible to anticipate that future caregiving responsibilities will interfere with work performance. You can't refuse, for example, to hire a female applicant based on the belief that she will have children in the future and need to take more time off.

The Supreme Court has made it clear that once an employee is pregnant you can't make negative employment decisions based on assumptions about how a pregnancy will affect performance. Similarly, you can't refuse to accommodate pregnant employees while you are accommodating other employees with disabling medical conditions.

Female employees with children sometimes feel as if they're treated with a double standard: viewed in the workplace as a "bad mother" for working hard, but also as a "bad employee" for devoting time to their family or needing to take time off to care for family members. Statistics show that females with children are hired and promoted at a lower rate than females without children and are offered $11,000 less pay; indeed, females with children are 79 percent less likely to be hired than females without children with equal qualifications, based on a catalyst survey.

Some employers have lost cases by assigning employees with caregiving responsibilities to less desirable positions, such as when an employer acts of its own accord to "protect" a new mother by assigning her to less challenging or demanding work, or transferring an employee to a new position so she has "more time to spend with family."

Surprisingly, a Work/Life Institute study has shown that male workers with children were treated better than female workers with children, such as where an employer refused to promote female employees to positions that required travel because it was unfair to her children. Women with children make seventy-three cents to a man's dollar. Single women with children make sixty cents to a man's dollar. Interestingly, single women with no children make ninety cents to a man's dollar.

Men suffer from caregiving discrimination also. Some men are refused leave for child-care responsibilities while honoring female employees' requests; the courts have universally found this to be illegal. Men who take parental leave are recommended for fewer rewards and viewed as less committed to the job.

Be aware that discrimination against employees for caregiving responsibilities associated with a disabled family member violates the ADA, as it constitutes discrimination based on association with an individual with disabilities.

You can, however, discipline new parents who miss work repeatedly for child-care obligations (a child who is not sick enough to be covered by FMLA, which requires a serious medical illness) where you can prove that you treated the parent the same as other employees with attendance problems.

Pregnancy Leave

Employees have a right to pregnancy leave under the FMLA, which covers the birth of a child of the employee (mother or father), as well as the placement of a child with the employee for adoption or foster care. FMLA is unpaid by law. Your organization can deduct the employee's pay for all the time not worked. The employee can also take all accrued paid vacation and sick leave and personal leave.

"We need to talk"

Another law, the Federal Pregnancy Discrimination Act, gives pregnant applicants and employees more rights than they had in 1978, when it was passed, but significantly fewer rights than employees protected by the ADA and the FMLA.

Tread carefully when one of your crew becomes pregnant. Don't fire, harass, tease, demote, or otherwise reassign her. Don't ask special questions about when she plans to return to work or how much time she plans on taking off. Just continue to ask all your employees what their plans are for the immediate future. If you've created a good relationship with your employees and kept the lines of communication open, she will come to you with her plans so that you can make your own.

Pregnant employees are not covered by the ADA, as it only applies to temporary disabilities. If the pregnancy occurs within the first year of employment, the FMLA doesn't cover them. For example, one court ruled that an employee who was excessively absent due to morning sickness could be terminated.

A normal pregnancy is not considered to be a disability. If, however, an employee needs to be on bed rest, hospitalized, or has other medical issues, she may qualify as *temporarily* disabled and be entitled to take time off under the FMLA, after her first year of employment, or after exhausting her company's sick leave policies. In California, however, employees are entitled to more rights than in other states. If your employee is disabled by pregnancy or childbirth, she is entitled to up to four months disability leave, even during her first year of employment.

> *"We need to talk"*
>
> Many other states have laws allowing workers to take time off from work to care for sick family members, attend school functions, or take a family member to medical appointments. These laws may cover smaller employers and different circumstances than the FMLA.

One of the most common questions employment lawyers receive is what to say to an employee who is pregnant or whom they suspect is pregnant. Basically, you cannot assume that pregnant employees are going to take any time off. You should not bring up the topic, except as you do for other employees when asking them about their future plans and goals.

While women taking no time off to have babies might be rare, I did have an attorney in my former law firm who was in the midst of an important criminal trial when her baby was due. A dedicated defense lawyer, she worked right up until one Friday night, when miraculously, the baby arrived during nonwork hours. On Monday morning, she was back in court. (I should add that, exhausted, she took an extended leave six months later.) The point is that we simply can't presume to know anyone else's plans about how she will take care of her family. It's important to remember that other employees also take time off, many times on short notice, for accidents, back surgery, heart attacks, and the like. Focusing on women and pregnancy leaves creates problems you don't want to have as a boss.

What does work is realizing that leaves for health problems and family illness are a common part of most workers' careers. Becoming too dependent upon any one worker or group of workers such that you can't afford to have them take time off is never smart. Even if you're a smaller business, there are scores of temporary firms of all sorts who offer employees to replace workers in almost any field. Have these kinds of resources tucked away in your pocket so that you won't have to scramble when the next leave request lands on your desk.

As covered in previous chapters, you should have regular performance meetings with all your employees. In these meetings, you should be asking all of them what their work plans and goals are for the next six months, one year, and five years.

Leave-Request Pointers

With the maze of leave requests and special rules, you may be feeling overwhelmed about this subject. Here are some practical pointers:

- Learn your own policies and procedures about leave. Find out what expert in your organization to go to with problems.
- When an employee first comes to you with a leave request, wait before answering. Ask open-ended questions but don't assure him that you'll take care of him. You may express concern about his health condition, but wait to offer leave until you know what's appropriate.
- Don't discriminate, harass, demote, or fire someone for taking a leave for her own health condition or the health condition of her family member for a leave allowed by the law or your policy. Make sure that other people don't treat her negatively either.

You have to treat her as if she'd never taken the leave and judge her work based on the amount of time she actually worked.

- Finally yet importantly, try to keep your head above the confusion and treat your employee like a human being. Don't forget how you might feel in a similar position.

While you should never promise any benefits until you know what you can actually deliver, remember some of the statistics from earlier in this chapter about how productive most disabled workers can be. In most organizations, employee loyalty is at an all-time low, due to layoffs, reorganizations, and the like. You would do well to earn your employees' trust by treating them well—within your employer's policy and the law—no matter how inconvenient their health problems might be. In the long run, such a posture will be well worth your while.

Make sure that you have coverage for all job types from other workers. You should never become too dependent upon one worker. You should cross-train people, utilize temporary workers, or have people share jobs so that you know you'll always be covered in case someone leaves or has to take time off. Health emergencies and family-care responsibilities are a reality in most workers' lives. Plan for these predictable surprises so that you won't be caught unprepared.

Sample Script   *"We need to talk"*

RORY: Susan, thanks for coming in. You know I like to do these quarterly reviews with everyone. How do you feel things are going here? (Asks same question of all employees.)

SUSAN: Things are going well.

RORY: Well, the one thing that I have on my list that I'd like to see improvement on is correspondence. You need to make sure that what goes out to clients is perfect. I appreciate how well you've been doing lately in returning client calls promptly.

SUSAN: Thanks. I'll work on that.

RORY: Any concerns about other parts of your work? What are your goals for the next few months and the year?

SUSAN: Well . . . I've been meaning to talk to you. I'm pregnant, and I'm going to be taking some time off.

RORY: Congratulations. When are you due?

SUSAN: March. I'd like to take three months under our policy and then come back full-time.

RORY: Well, let's look at the calendar and make a plan.

Employee Communication Don'ts	Employee Communication Dos
Discriminate or harass employees who take health-related time off.	*Treat all workers with respect.*
Ignore your policies.	*Learn about your policies.*
Assume pregnant women or workers with family will be less committed.	*Let employees tell you what they need.*
Assume perfect attendance.	*Plan for leave requests.*

Chapter 7

How to Talk about Hygiene, Dress, and Hairdos

TODD JAMES GLUMLY stacked and restacked the already neat pile of files on his desk. He took a deep gulp of his cold decaf coffee and sighed.

"Why me?" he fumed. "Why do I have to get all the sticky issues? Just for once I wish I could get the easy ones."

He picked up his file on his assistant Carol and skimmed the all-too-familiar e-mail trail of comments about her. He'd intercepted a long string of rude back-and-forths between the guys in his department, such as

"Man, did you see Carol today? Do you think she has anything under that skirt?"

"Under? How could she? Nothing would fit under it!"

"How about that top? She was leaning over my desk to give me a file and I thought those hooters were going to fall right out!"

"And that eyeliner! Do you think she uses a shovel to put it on? Princess Dracula!"

And on and on.

He'd noticed her attire himself, of course. More suitable for salsa dancing than for the office, but he just didn't know how to deal with the situation. Today she had on a micro-mini leather skirt, fishnet stockings, and a blouse that went right up to her neck but was see-through! How could she have worked this long without anyone telling her what constituted proper office attire? And her last job had been at a law firm?

The problem was that she was a crackerjack assistant. She was in at 7:30 A.M. and always willing to stay late. She returned reports early and error-free, cleaned out the file room without being asked, and was friendly to everyone. However, her wardrobe was creating problems.

Why did he want to be a director, anyway, Todd wondered? In the six months since he'd been promoted, he felt more like a high school guidance counselor than a manager. He had to talk to her today! He took another gulp of coffee and clutched his file as he lurched down the hall to her desk—without a clue of what he was going to say.

Your Rights and Responsibilities as a Manager

Clearly, one of your responsibilities as a manager is to create an environment that's safe and where employees are able to focus on getting their work done. If someone's dressing in a way that's distracting to the rest of the workforce, it may be difficult for other employees to work as productively as they could. You have a right, and indeed, an obligation as a manager to step in and make sure that you create an environment that's safe and productive for everyone.

But Isn't That Harassment or Discrimination?

Many managers, especially male ones, are afraid to confront women about their clothes, makeup, or hair. While you may—if you're in this situation—want to consult with HR for some coaching before you approach this issue, you clearly have to discuss this in a way that is not harassment.

What you can't do is stereotype. Stereotyping *can* be a subtle form of discrimination and harassment. We all have some biases about one group or another. Most stereotypes are probably unconscious; they may even be well-meaning. Stereotyping is so common, in fact, that for years it was not recognized as the basis for a discrimination lawsuit.

That changed in 1989, when the U.S. Supreme Court decided a case against PriceWaterhouse. Ann Hopkins was one of 88 candidates for partnership in the Big Eight accounting firm. She brought more business to the firm than any other candidate. But she was not chosen for partner. The firm said she needed to "walk more femininely, talk more femininely, dress more femininely, wear makeup, have [her] hair styled, and wear jewelry." The partners complained that she used too much profanity "for a lady." One said she needed "a course in charm school."

The Supreme Court found these comments showed that stereotyped views of women were being used as criteria for partnership. If the defendants had used legitimate business standards, Hopkins would have made partner since she was an excellent employee.

Men are also protected against discrimination or harassment based on stereotypes about who is a "real man," which can include comments or coaching about dress or hair. In one case, a man worked as a waiter in a Mexican restaurant. He was heterosexual, but his supervisor and coworkers barraged him with insults every day, calling him "her," "girl," "whore," or saying he "walked like a woman." In ruling that the waiter could sue for sexual harassment, the court relied on the PriceWaterhouse case, finding that harassing a man because he does not live up to a societal stereotype of virility is every bit as illegal as discriminating against a woman who is perceived not to be "feminine" enough.

The one exception to this kind of stereotyping is if you can show a strong business-related need for makeup or certain clothes. Actors, singer, dancers and other entertainers, cosmetologists, cosmetics salespeople, and beauticians might be included.

For other jobs, dress, appearance, and grooming codes are usually permissible, even if they treat men and women differently. For instance, an employer may impose different hair length requirements on men and women, and may require men but not women to wear neckties. But in California, a state law says employers can't make women wear skirts!

A "good grooming" standard for both sexes would be fine. But a dress or appearance standard cannot impose substantially different *burdens* on men and women. So a restaurant can require men and women to wear different uniforms, but it cannot require only women to wear uniforms. An airline can require all flight attendants to wear contact lenses, but not just women. In fact, a federal appeals court recently ruled in favor of a class action by former United Airlines flight attendants who had been fired for exceeding the weight tables. Women were judged by weight tables for a medium frame; men were judged by weight tables based on a large frame.

"We need to talk"

Beware. If you're only counseling women and not men about their grooming or professional appearance, there may be ground for a claim of sex discrimination.

However, you can, for example, have a dress or grooming standard that includes hiding such things as tattoos, hickeys, or piercings, especially in public contact positions. Again, make sure that you impose the same rules for both sexes.

Employees have tried to attack dress codes in all kinds of creative ways. Employers have a lot of leeway in deciding what dress is appropriate for the workplace. In one interesting case, a computer programmer was fired because he wore Hawaiian shirts to work instead of the business attire called for in the dress code. He sued under the ADA, claiming that, because of a prior auto accident, he could not wear a tie, and he had a doctor's note supporting his need to wear shirts that were loose around the clavicle. A federal appeals court affirmed the decision to throw out his case without trial, finding that the inability to wear a tie was not a disability!

Gender Identity

This sexual stereotyping in terms of dress and hair has recently been extended to transsexuals. Although federal law has banned sex discrimination since 1964, federal courts of appeal have uniformly held that Congress did not intend the term *sex* to include transsexuals. State and federal courts and state legislators, however, have started to recognize that sex discrimination can involve gender stereotypes about so-called "masculine" or "feminine" traits. In 2005, a pre-operative transsexual man alleged that his promotion to sergeant in the Cincinnati Police Department was revoked in part because he lived as a man at work but as a woman when off-duty. The jury agreed, finding that he was the victim of sexual stereotyping, and awarded him $320,000 in damages. The trial judge tacked on $25,000 in court costs and nearly $530,000 in attorneys' fees.

Gender identity is a protected characteristic in California, Connecticut, the District of Columbia, Hawaii, Maine, Massachusetts, Minnesota, New Jersey, New Mexico, New York, Rhode Island, and Washington.

The Human Rights Campaign provides some suggestions for understanding of transgendered employees:

- Gender nonconformity is an expression of natural human diversity, which has occurred throughout history—although it has often been suppressed and continues to be misunderstood. Today, modern medicine has expanded personal choice in this area, so this aspect of human diversity is becoming more visible.
- Employers should not casually discard the investment they have made in a transgendered employee. Consider the employee's experience, history, and overall work record.
- Workers who are valued and treated with respect are more loyal and committed to their jobs. By treating the transgendered employee with respect and understanding, you build that trust and commitment. Moreover, other employees watch how management treats particular workers, and they make decisions about loyalty to the team and the employer based on what they see. Fairness matters.
- Any awkwardness or concerns with initial appearance and demeanor issues tend to resolve themselves with time.

Management concerns about adverse customer and coworker reactions should be evaluated in light of this fact.

- Bear in mind that this employee likely has thought long and hard about coming out as transgendered. This is not a decision people reach without much soul-searching.
- There is no evidence that allowing an employee to transition will open the floodgates to nonconformity. Developing an appropriate management process, however, will make it easier next time, if there is a next time.

Many managers continue to have this wrong-headed idea that somehow even mentioning hair, clothes, or bad breath would be harassment. Not true. The key is to focus on the relationship between professional dress, hair, or other issues, and work. It's helpful if your company has a dress code, but even if it doesn't, you can talk about what's professional dress and grooming for your setting.

It may be difficult for you to seek out individuals for this if you haven't talked about it in a general way. A good way to start then would be to have a meeting with your staff to talk about standards for professional dress and grooming, and then follow up with your staff individually if things don't change. Some of the larger department and specialty stores actually have experts who will come in and talk with your people about this if you need extra help. Especially with the rise of "business casual" days and codes, employees these days may be confused about what to wear.

General Rules for Talking about Dress or Grooming Issues

Before launching into a conversation with an employee whom you believe to have dress or grooming issues, consider whether you can meet these general rules:

- Have a dress and grooming code. It will be far easier to talk in the context of a specific code, and that way your employees are less likely to consider you discriminatory or to feel as if they're being singled out in some way. If you don't have one, work with HR or an employment attorney to create one as a part of your employee manual.

- Focus on performance. How does this particular dress or grooming issue impact performance? If it doesn't, *stop*! You may be creating privacy, discrimination, or other issues. For example, does the dress or grooming issue create a distraction for other employees or customers? Does the perfume or body odor create triggers for other employees' allergies? These are legitimate reasons to require a different dress or grooming. You have a right and, indeed, an obligation to try and create a productive workplace for everyone.

- Seek coaching from HR or your employment attorney. These conversations can be difficult. You need to role-play with someone else first, if possible. Write out what you plan to say. Be prepared. Otherwise, it's easy to get tongue-tied on this difficult topic.

- Talk in private. These conversations can be very embarrassing to the employee who frequently has no idea how he's affecting other people. Make sure that you give him the privacy he needs and deserves.

- Be specific. You need to tell the employee specifically what is wrong with what she's wearing or doing and what would make the situation comply with your policy. Don't assume that she can guess what you mean and what you want without some very specific suggestions from you.
- Don't beat around the bush. Get to the point and tell the truth fast.
- Don't stereotype or discriminate. Be careful if you're only counseling women that you're not requiring certain standards about the notions of masculinity or femininity unless you're in the entertainment industry and can justify a difference based on that.
- As with any emotional issue, give the employee time to think about and respond to what you've said. Listen so that you can hear opportunities for joint problem solving.

What If They Resist? Turning Adversaries into Partners

Sometimes employees take a stand over things that most bosses find inconsequential; hair and clothes sometimes top the list. If your employee chooses to do this, it's a good chance to learn an important skill: turning adversaries into partners.

I once coached a manager, Tim, who had an employee named Jack who was covered with tattoos. The company dress policy required tattoos to be covered.

Jack would comply for a while but would gradually sink back into defiance with his shirt sleeves creeping up so his tattoos were displayed. Jack was an otherwise energetic employee at Tim's restaurant, in an industry where good employees are scarce.

When a boss-employee conflict like this persists, there is often a back-story to it. The real problem wasn't Tim versus Jack, but rather it was something about how both of them were feeling about deeper issues in the present moment, and how they were treating each other.

The last conversation had gotten hot, with both Tim and Jack yelling at each other. When Tim called, I recommended that he let the matter drop for that day and take a time out to calm down and cool off. Tim didn't want to leave Jack on the floor in a short-sleeved shirt all day—in violation of their policy—but he grudgingly agreed.

What Tim needed to do was to stop treating Jack like an adversary and start treating him as a partner. Issues like this pop up in everyone's life. In fact, many conflict specialists recommend focusing on turning an *adversary* into a *partner*—viewing the *problem* as a common enemy to be tamed by both of you. If you can imagine yourself on the same side as your employee and plop the problem on the opposite side of the table or desk from the two of you, and, if you can convince the other person to go along, you'll have a leg up.

Before you do that, you need to make the other person feel like he has really been heard, something everyone craves. Frequently, when you can hear what your employee is complaining about, at both a superficial level as well as the deeper one, the problem either resolves itself or disappears.

I kept repeating the *partner, partner, listen, listen* mantra, and explaining the concept to Tim. He sat Jack down the next day to try to have a different kind of conversation.

Tim started off by apologizing for blowing up the day before. "I'm sorry that I yelled yesterday but I was really frustrated. We've talked about this issue of what you wear many times, and I really need you to comply with our dress code, but it doesn't seem to be happening. You're a good worker, and I want to keep you here. You say that you will comply, but then it doesn't happen. What do you think causes that?"

Rather than just ordering Jack to comply with the dress code once more, Tim invited him to disclose the deeper story.

Jack looked down and started mumbling, "I know, but it's just hard for me to be here all the time, I mean no one knows me and. . . ."

Tim, as instructed by me, looked for an opening to get Jack to explain more. "When you say that you don't feel that anyone here really knows you, what do you mean?"

Jack looked up and started directly at Tim. "Well! You don't think I want to be a waiter forever do you?"

Tim then used one of the techniques I'd suggested, continuing to ask open-ended questions and making empathetic noises until Jack calmed down. Sometimes being listened to without judgment but with full attention may be all someone needs.

What emerged of Jack's story was that he really didn't want to wait tables forever; he was a singer and songwriter and wanted to make a living that way. He chafed under the restrictions of working in a place where "no one knew him," and exposing his tattoos was a way of letting people know that he saw himself as more than a server.

I had asked Tim to imagine that he were Jack. After hearing his story, Tim could more easily do that. In my conflict workshops, I always require students to use this technique to switch sides and tell the story of the conflict from the other person's point of view. While students initially resist these kinds of "acting" exercises, these activities are always revealing and helpful in allowing employers and employees to move beyond a conflict that's "stuck."

Seeing Jack's side made Tim feel a bit uncomfortable, but also less entitled and less inclined to climb into the ring and defend the dress code. If he did that, he would just push Jack into his corner of the ring, leaving him with no choice but to continue to defend his right to dress how he pleased. That result would not serve anyone.

Understanding what someone is really feeling or thinking beneath the surface of what they initially say is a crucial step to resolving conflicts with employees—or anyone else. There is power in your own attitude. Even if someone initially resists your invitation to begin a dialogue, rather than a debate, you don't have to react in kind. You can continue to say and do things that turn you and your employee into partners, not adversaries. All it takes is persistence in trying to understand the other person's point of view and reflect it back so that she feels that someone understands and appreciates the problem. We can choose to view this as an interesting challenge or a pesky chore.

Tim continued to listen and ask Jack about his singing, his career goals and frustrations, and the series of other jobs he'd had while trying to make a living and continue writing songs. When he seemed to have no more left to say, I had Tim ask what I call the "clincher" question: "What would be the best possible outcome for you for this issue?"

This question took Jack aback and stopped him in the middle of his litany of complaints. Until then, he'd not been looking at the big picture, but only the current annoyance about the dress code. He sat still for a long time. "Well," he said finally, blushing, "I'd really like to sing and play in the bar on my nights off."

Now it was Tim's turn to be taken aback. In his wildest dreams, he never would have imagined that suggested outcome. "Well," he said finally. "Let me think about it, but my initial reaction is that sounds like a fine idea. I've wanted to find some live music for the bar. I would need, however, for you to comply with the dress code when you're waiting on tables."

"You mean it," said Jack. "Right on!"

Not all boss-employee clashes play out this easily, of course, but the same steps can be used in virtually any employee conflict. Try this format:

1. Calm yourself down so you can think. Ignore whatever distraction the employee is throwing at you.
2. Focus on the big picture. What is the outcome you really need and want?
3. Find the employee's back-story. Gradually reveal your own.
4. Ask open-ended questions. Use this format: listen, question, listen, question, and listen.
5. Imagine yourself in his shoes. Articulate the employee's deeper issues either to yourself or to him, if appropriate.
6. Brainstorm a solution that meets everyone's needs.

Additional Techniques to Use with Angry Employees

Because hair, dress, and hygiene are so personal, sometimes employees express emotions beyond what the situation seems to merit. Before you impose discipline or terminations, consider these additional techniques.

First, allow the employee to express anger and resentment appropriately. Let the person speak these feelings until he is finished.

135

Acknowledge his feelings, which means listening and empathizing without excuses or explanations. He may be trying to work out issues about the past, meaning that this situation and/or you remind him of some past upset, and he's taking it out on you. Reassure him that you will not allow the past to repeat itself in this relationship. If you let the person completely express all of his feelings, anger and resentment will eventually turn into appreciation.

In general, appreciation is a good way to keep employees from turning into pains. Frequently ask them, "What can I do that would make you feel more appreciated today?" Can you imagine how you'd feel if *your* boss asked you this question instead of taking you for granted?

Consider, also, the power of silence. If you're on the receiving end of an employee harangue, and you've never used silence to make a point, you don't understand how powerful this communication tool can be. Being able to use the sound of silence is one of the greatest conversational arts.

Our ability to be quiet may confirm that we are intensely interested in what is being said. It can also show that we have great integrity and will not be brought into conversations that could be demeaning. Ben Franklin said, "Remember not only to say the right thing in the right place, but far more difficult still, to leave unsaid the wrong thing at the tempting moment." Silence allows us to keep a secret, to serve as peacemaker, and to learn the deeper meaning about what is being said.

Have you ever been in a conversation in which all you were waiting for was for the speaker to pause, so that you could interject your reply? Instead of allowing ourselves to pause and absorb what has been said, we start preparing how we want to vocalize our thoughts as soon as the speaker stops talking. This is not listening; it is merely practicing our next speech.

Realize that there will always be some people who misunderstand or misinterpret your silence. Some employees will take your pause as a time to jump into the conversation by engaging their mouth. When we do speak, our brains should be fully engaged so that our words are clear and easily understood. Otherwise, our words are only noise pollution.

"We need to talk"

> Silence is a powerful sword. We can use silence to increase our understanding and learn more about the people around us. When used out of compassion, it can show that we care deeply enough to listen with the intent to understand.

However, the other side of the silence sword can cut through the air when our intent is to hurt someone or let someone know we are displeased. Be careful not to do this with employees, who are usually much attuned to the power differential between them and the boss. Dead silence can cause a conversation to feel heavy, because the speaker may not know whether he or she was heard or understood. The art of silence is learned. When we are accustomed to noise, we may mistake silence for lack of understanding.

How loud is your silence when you are speaking with the people you supervise? Is your silence allowing you to hit your mark and better understand your employees, or are you using it to dismiss, intimidate, or punish passive-aggressively? Be aware of your intentions with this tactic.

So the next time you're confronted by a really troublesome employee, try silence. Simply let the person talk, vent, even rage to her heart's content. If she is behaving like a snarling, snapping, sniping pit bull, realize that most of these "pit-bulls" are like balloons full of hot air: if you simply allow them to go on long enough, they'll eventually deflate.

If the employee pauses, ask another open-ended question, starting with who, what, where, and when. If you can't think of anything else to say, you can always just simply ask, "And then what happened?" Every time the employee runs through the problems at hand, you can help her blow off the anger until it disappears. In between the tirades, use the power of silence.

Sample Script

"We need to talk"

After stopping in at HR for some coaching and guidance, Todd called Carol into his office. After shutting the door, he took a deep breath and began.

TODD: You know, Carol, how much I and the other team members value your work here. Your energy and enthusiasm, as well as your willingness to work late whenever necessary, has helped us be one of the most effective teams in the company. (Start with understanding and appreciation.)

CAROL: Well, thank you, I enjoy working with you guys.

TODD: I do have one problem that I've been meaning to talk to you about and, I must admit, it's not an easy subject for me to raise. (Get to the point; tell the truth fast.)

CAROL: A problem . . . ?

TODD: Yes. You know that we do have a business casual dress code here, but there still are some guidelines that we have to follow. We've never really discussed it in this department, and, because you're the only woman, I wanted to talk to you in private about it. (Outline the general rules, policy, or standards for the discussion.)

CAROL: Yes, I've always appreciated how we can dress however we want to here.

TODD: And, yes, I understand, but that's just the problem. Unfortunately, your style is a bit different from what works for our office. (Listens for bridging cues to follow her own story.) We need to come up with a modification of your style that's more consistent with our environment. (Frames the problem as a joint issue that they can work on together.)

CAROL: I'm not sure what you mean.

TODD: Well, as I said, this is hard for me, but I have discussed it with Helen in HR and she gave me some guidelines for women that they came out with a few years ago. They cover things such as skirt length and blouses. Here's a copy for you, and Helen said that she'd be glad to talk to you. I'm afraid that some of the outfits you wear are just too distracting for the workplace. We do value your work and want to do everything we can to continue to make this a productive environment for you and everyone else. I would like to know your thoughts about this, either now, or, if you want to take some time to think about it and get back to me, please let me know when you can talk. (Give her space and time to collect herself.)

CAROL: I guess I'll think about it and get back to you.

Employee Conversation Don'ts	Employee Conversation Dos
Fail to talk about hair, dress, and hygiene.	*Confront these issues skillfully.*
Confront women and not men.	*Try to have gender-neutral standards.*
Talk too much.	*Listen to an employee's concerns to discover the deeper issue.*

"We need to talk"

Chapter 8

How to Respond to Complaints about Discrimination, Threats, Dishonesty, or Unsafe Working Conditions

MAURICE WILSON STARED at the young woman sitting in front of him and blinked. Had he heard her correctly? Sherri was accusing him of discrimination against women. Hadn't he been the one to promote more women than any other general manager in the hotel? Hadn't he mentored, hired, and advised more women over the course of his career than anyone in the industry? Known for his gift of gab, for once, Maurice had no idea what to say.

This chapter will cover some of the more common complaints in the workplace. Be aware, however, that some federal laws on these issues do not apply if you work for an employer with fewer than fifteen (in some cases) or fifty (in other situations) employees. Also, government employees are frequently subject to different rules, and union contracts may provide additional wrinkles. What is offered below is meant to be a general educational overview of the problem. As always, you need to research the laws and policies that govern your particular state and employer and you may need to consult HR or an attorney.

Illegal Harassment and Discrimination: True Legal Violations

Using the terms *illegal harassment* or *discrimination* implies that there's such a thing as legal harassment and, in fact, there is. Harassment and discrimination claims remain the most common legal complaints in most workplaces.

How Common Are Discrimination Complaints?

How common are discrimination and harassment complaints? Still startlingly common, unfortunately. The EEOC received a total of 82,792 private sector discrimination charge filings last fiscal year. This is the highest volume of incoming charges since 2002 and the largest annual increase (9 percent) since the early 1990s. The EEOC recovered $345 million in monetary relief for job bias victims.

In 2007, allegations of discrimination based on race, retaliation, and sex were the most frequently filed charges, continuing a long-term trend, but nearly all major charge categories showed double-digit percentage increases from the prior year. The agency report speculated that the jump in charge filings may be due to a combination of factors, including greater awareness of the law, changing economic conditions, and increased diversity and demographic shifts in the labor force.

In 2007, retaliation was, for the first time, the second highest charge category (behind race), surpassing sex-based charges in total filings with EEOC offices nationwide. Since the EEOC became operational in 1965, race has been the most frequently filed charge.

Issues such as pregnancy discrimination and sexual harassment also trended upward at both the EEOC and state and local Fair Employment Practices Agencies.

For example, during 2007, pregnancy charges surged to a record high of 5,587, up 14 percent. Sexual harassment filings increased for the first time since 2000, numbering 12,510, up 4 percent. Additionally, a record 16 percent of sexual harassment charges were filed by men, up from 9 percent in the early 1990s.

Age cases had the largest annual increase since 2002, up 15 percent. In general, age discrimination is the fastest-growing class of cases in the federal courts these days. Why? All of the baby boomers, of course. They're all over the age of forty and accustomed to asserting their rights. Last but not least, the report indicated that religion cases were up to record high levels, doubling since 1992.

These statistics don't even reflect the number of private suits that have been filed but those numbers are also at historic highs. What these statistics make apparent is that there is, unfortunately, a good chance of someone complaining about these matters. Being prepared for your first (or next) such complaint is key.

Preparing Your Company for Complaints

As with other issues discussed in earlier chapters, it helps to talk to all your employees about discrimination before they come to you with a complaint. At a minimum, review your company's policies about discrimination and ethics codes at least once a year. If you have an inside or outside training department, bring a representative from that department in to do training reviews at least once every two years. If you do, you'll gradually reduce the amount of claims, as well as assure your employees that you take these matters seriously.

If you do bring someone in to do training, introduce the instructors yourself and say something like this: "As you know, these are important matters for our organization. We take complaints about discrimination, harassment, ethics, or safety violations very seriously. I want you all to be aware of what acceptable behavior is in our workplace. Please know that I'm available to talk about any concerns you might have about these matters."

It might seem counterintuitive for you to actually encourage people to come to you with complaints. You might even feel that you already have enough employee complaints! Yet, believe me, complaints are the good news. If employees perceive problems in any of these areas, you want them to come to you first, not go over your head or to an outside agency. You don't want to learn about a legal problem when the subpoena lands on your desk!

> ### "We need to talk"
>
> If you have these kinds of sessions with your employees on a regular basis, they'll be more likely to trust you when they do have a complaint, to come to you first, and to be more reasonable in working out the problem. Create an environment where you're safe to confront.

Many legal tangles can be avoided if managers follow these principles. Most employees actually don't want to go through all the hassle of finding an attorney and suing their employer. And most plaintiffs' (employees') attorneys won't take the case unless they think they can win. If you've created an environment where employees feel free to come to you, be listened to, and have their issues addressed appropriately, you will most likely head things off at the pass.

This is another area of the law where you need to have an expert to whom you can go with specific questions. If you have a large HR department, it will most likely include someone who deals with employee relationship issues such as these. If you don't, you'll need to find an employment lawyer to help you when the need arises. It's good to interview someone ahead of time and have her available before you need her. Most things can be fixed, if you call an expert soon enough.

What constitutes illegal harassment and discrimination seems to be the subject of endless workplace confusion. This is because the law sets a floor for workplace behavior. I call it the "red zone." Many organizations have a policy that is stricter than the law requires. Further, every court in the country has held that companies may have a stricter policy and can discipline people who violate that policy even if the behavior in no way violates the law. Behavior that merely "offends" someone, however, is not a legal problem. Much different standards from that must be met before harassment or discrimination crosses legal boundaries.

Harassment and Discrimination Legal Standards

Federal laws prohibit discrimination, harassment, and retaliation because of

- Sex or gender;
- Age;
- Race and color;
- Religion;
- National origin;

- Citizenship;
- Physical disability (including emotional or mental disabilities);
- Pregnancy;
- Veteran/military status; and
- Family and medical leave.

These are often referred to as "protected characteristics." You may have heard the term *protected group* as in, "women are a protected group" or "African Americans are a protected group," but that terminology is actually incorrect. What's protected is the characteristic, not the group. We all have a gender, and so we're all protected from discrimination because of our gender. We all have skin color, so we're all protected from discrimination based on the color of our skin.

Harassment because of sex includes the following:

- Sexual harassment;
- Gender harassment;
- Same-sex harassment; and
- Harassment based on pregnancy.

If you live in California and some other states, you have some additional protection. California has perhaps the strictest laws in the country on these issues and also prohibits discrimination, harassment, and retaliation because of

- Status as a domestic violence victim;
- Medical condition or genetic characteristic;
- Ancestry;
- Marital status;

- Sexual orientation; and
- Childbirth and related medical conditions.

Many managers are confused about the difference between harassment, discrimination, and retaliation. Harassment protection is not, in fact, based on a new law but has been around since the 1964 Civil Rights Act. It is one kind of discrimination.

"We need to talk"

The first Supreme Court case to consider the harassment issue involved a bank teller who had sex with a bank officer for years. She argued in court that she felt coerced to have a relationship with her boss in order to keep her job. The Supreme Court agreed that her situation could constitute illegal sexual harassment.

Discrimination is an adverse job action taken by a supervisor because of the individual's protected characteristics (as listed above). Adverse job actions include failures to hire or promote, firing or layoffs, cuts in pay, denials of salary increase, and changing other terms or conditions of employment such as hours or vacation time because of a protected characteristic.

Retaliation is an action taken against someone for protesting, complaining, or cooperating in the investigation of discrimination or harassment. This action can include any adverse job action or physical retaliation such as physical threats, assault or battery, destruction of personal property, or stalking.

Types of Harassment

Harassment can be an adverse job action that takes the form of a physical, visual, or verbal action. In the "red zone" there is true illegal harassment, known as *quid pro quo* ("this for that"). This takes the form of "You have to date me to get this job" or "You have to have sex with me to get this promotion." This type of harassment usually involves a colleague or superior leveraging job favors for sexual favors. The harasser is someone who actually has the power to grant such favors, either by express or implied threats. Quid pro quo can also be implied by repeated propositions. Your employee must, however, show that the harassment had some impact on his job, such as that he was denied an annual pay increase, laid off, or forced to quit. Usually, this means that the harassment must have been severe or pervasive.

Illegal Retaliation

Illegal retaliation is another type of harassment in which a supervisor, peer, subordinate, or outsider retaliates against the employee for a claim. Retaliation can take many forms, such as a demotion, poor performance appraisals, bad job assignments, termination threats, or violence.

For example, in one retaliation claim, an employee at a high-tech company alleged that he was retaliated against because he had testified as a witness in a racial discrimination case. He claimed that the VP involved in the case "belittled" him in meetings after he testified. While this might have been a good claim of retaliation, investigation revealed that this particular VP treated other employees exactly the same way and that the employee himself had been treated in the same manner *before* the lawsuit.

Sexual Favoritism

Another type of harassment is illegal sexual favoritism. If the situation amounts to isolated instances of management giving favorable treatment to paramours, then in most cases, it isn't illegal, although it probably violates your organization's policy. If sexual favoritism is widespread in the company, that's likely to be illegal.

Hostile Environment

Finally yet importantly, is illegal hostile environment. This is the accusation that many people hurl around carelessly. Many people seem to think that they are in a hostile environment if someone's behavior offends them. Not true.

In order to prove a true hostile environment, an employee must show that the behavior was discriminating or sexually harassing in tone and nature. This means that harassment is based on one of the specific characteristics as listed above. Contrary to popular belief, in most states there's no such thing as illegal "general" harassment. If it's not tied to one of these protected classifications, it is not illegal. However, general harassment may violate criminal laws (assault, stalking, threats, and so on) if it is severe enough.

Second, an employee must prove that the behavior is unwelcome by the victim, meaning that the employee didn't encourage the behavior or participate in it. Third, in order to prove illegal harassment, an employee must show that it was severe, meaning that it interfered with work. Last but not least, an employee has to prove that the employer knew, or should have known, and did nothing. An employee must be able to prove all four of these factors in order to prove illegal harassment under the law.

Religious Discrimination

Most employers can recognize discrimination based on race, sex, age, or disability but may become confused when faced with a claim of religious discrimination so that issue deserves a special note.

The law protects employees of every religion, including atheists, from discrimination because of their beliefs. Employers can't refuse to hire or promote someone because of their religion. Be careful, also, of recruiting all your employees from your own religion.

What about religious expression in the workplace? This is a complicated issue. Basically, employees have the right to religious expression, within reasonable limits, but can't proselytize or try to convert others. An employee might be able to display a small religious symbol at her workspace. Employees cannot, however, harass people about their religion or try to convert them or read religious books aloud.

Employees must also be "reasonably accommodated," in order to practice their religion. If their religion requires employees to wear certain types of clothing or fast on certain days, you have to find a way to allow those practices.

You also have to allow your employees a reasonable amount of time off, with or without pay, for religious holidays, just as you would allow other employees' personal time off. In addition, you have to accommodate the schedules of employees who can't work Saturdays or Sundays because of religious observances. For example, if you've never before required an employee to work weekends, you can't all of a sudden require it if your employees need those days off for religious reasons.

If you need employees to work on Saturdays, you need to accommodate those who practice their religion on those days and make them exempt from that requirement, if you can do so "reasonably." The same with hiring: You can't refuse to hire someone who can't work on Saturdays for religious reasons if you have other people who can cover that shift. If you need someone to work every Saturday, and the person that you're interviewing can't, you probably don't have to hire him if you can't reasonably fill that need with other members of your workforce.

Treating employees differently because of religion may seem wrong when there's been so much emphasis on treating people consistently, but free expression of religion is strongly protected in this country. If employees complain that you're offering certain employees special status, you just have to explain to them that you will handle their religious expression in the same way when and if they assert religious claims.

Military/Veteran Status

With a nation at war, claims and confusion about how to handle military status at work are becoming more common. Federal law prohibits discrimination against military veterans and reservists. The Selective Training and Service Act of 1940 provided the first such protection. The Act was amended during the Vietnam era. The Uniformed Services Employment and Re-employment Rights Act (USERRA) added new rights.

USERRA prohibits employers from denying employment, re-employment, retention, promotion, or any employment benefit to anyone on the basis that the person is a member of, has applied to join, is a veteran of, or performs service obligations for the military. You can, however, refuse to hire, promote, or otherwise discriminate against someone in this category if you can prove that you would have taken the same action even if the person were not a veteran. If you can prove, for example, job misconduct, lack of qualifications, or fraud, you can discriminate against a vet or someone currently serving.

Under USERRA, you also have to allow workers to take leave for military service and not create any negative consequences for them if they do so. Also, you have to give them full credit for the time they spend in uniform in terms of seniority, pension plans, and other benefits.

When soldiers return from duty, with a few exceptions, you must reinstate them to their old job or an equivalent position. Under USERRA regulations issued in 2005, known as the "escalator" principle, you may even be required to put them in a job they would have had if they'd remained continuously employed. If they've been on leave for more than thirty days, you can't fire them without cause for one year after they come back.

Most states also have laws protecting soldiers and returning veterans in the same way.

Sexual Orientation

While there's no federal law prohibiting discrimination based on sexual orientation, some states and cities do prohibit discrimination against gay men, lesbians, and bisexuals. Currently, sixteen states and the District of Columbia prohibit discrimination by private employers on the basis of sexual orientation. Nearly 200 cities and counties have ordinances that ban discrimination and harassment based on sexual orientation.

An executive order issued in 1998 prohibits discrimination based on sexual orientation in federal executive branch civilian employment.

Gender Identity

While there's no federal law banning discrimination against the transgendered (transsexuals, cross-dressers, intersexed people, and others who fall outside the traditional notions of gender identity), some states do define gender identity as a protected characteristic.

Harassment or Discrimination under Your Organization's Policies

Employers can, and frequently do, prohibit all harassment under their own policies, not just harassment based on race, sex, or other protected characteristic. This may include all behavior that is disrespectful. Check your organization's policies, which should be posted in the workplace, in your employee manual, or on your website. You may be surprised to learn how broad it is. A typical statement might be as follows:

✳   ✳   ✳

Workplace Harassment

ABC Company is committed to providing all employees with a work environment free from hostility and harassment and provides this policy to express that commitment. We recognize that harassment in any form destroys morale, impairs productivity, and is not permissible in a productive, cooperative environment.

ABC Company will carefully investigate and vigorously enforce all reported violations of this policy. Harassment by management or coworkers including but not limited to harassment based upon race, sex, color, religion, national origin, age, disability, or veteran status, whether verbally or physically, will not be tolerated. Harassing language or actions are not only a violation of company policy, but may constitute an illegal act. We will comply with all federal, state, and/or local laws.

ABC Company prohibits workplace harassment of every kind, including sexually related conduct of a physical, verbal, or visual nature that creates an intimidating, hostile, seductive, or offensive work environment; unwanted touching, patting, grabbing, repeated objectionable sexual flirtations, propositions, suggestive comments, or lewd jokes and display in the workplace of sexually explicit objects, drawings, or photos. Of course, ABC Company also prohibits any employee from making unwelcome sexual advances or requests for sexual favors when submission or rejection of such conduct is used as the basis for employment-related decisions.

* * *

Statements that an employer prohibits harassment "in any form" have become quite common in most workplaces. These statements can provide an employee with powerful ammunition when they complain about harassment that may be borderline under the law.

If you're still confused about what really crosses the line into legal or policy violations, check out the following list from one of our clients:

* * *

Note: the following list of examples does not include all potential legal or policy violations.

Examples of Legal or Policy Violations
- Objectionable comments about a person's age, race, skin color, national origin, ethnic background, religion, gender,

marital status, disability or medical problem, age, or veteran status

- Repeated and unwelcome requests for a date
- Racial, sexual orientation, sexist, age-related, or sexual jokes or comments
- Referring to a coworker in demeaning language (such as "babe," "girl"/"boy," "broad," "colored," "cripple," "grandpa," "pops")
- Unwelcome following of a person inside or outside of work
- Making sexual gestures
- Wearing or displaying the Confederate flag
- Accessing or displaying sexual or racial pictures, cartoons, or websites
- Unwelcome touching of a person's hair, clothing, or body
- Unwelcome kissing, hugging, or patting
- Wearing or displaying hate-related symbols (such as a swastika)
- Restraining or blocking the path of a person
- Touching oneself in a way that is suggestive in view of a coworker
- Spreading rumors about a coworker's sex life, including affairs, marital status, or sexual orientation
- Repeatedly leering at a coworker
- Making sexually suggestive facial expressions (winking, blowing kisses)
- Treating someone differently after a legally protected medical or family leave
- Neglecting to consider a woman with small children for a job that requires travel

- Refusing to consider older candidates because they are "overqualified"

* * *

There is always the question, of course, of whether your organization is willing to enforce the law and their policies. As a manager, you have a legal obligation to follow the law and intervene when you see or hear of behavior that violates the law. In addition, you have a fiduciary obligation to your organization to follow its policies.

Values Violations

In addition to formal policy statements, many organizations also have values statements. While these may seem as familiar and useless as wallpaper, you would be well advised to check them out, read them, and ponder whether any of the behavior you're allowing your employees to engage in seems to violate the organization's stated values. These values may include things such as "people are our most important resource," "we respect all our employees," and so on.

Although it's easy to become cynical about whether the organization really stands behind and intends to enforce these messages, a good manager has internalized those kinds of values and makes sure that they are exhibiting behavior consistent with those values, as well as ensuring that their employees do the same.

Whistle-Blower Protection

You can't fire or discipline an employee for reporting a violation of the law, for refusing to violate a law, or for refusing to violate public policy. One of the first whistle-blower cases involved a man who was called to testify against his employer in an IRS case. His boss came in the day before he was scheduled to testify and said he should lie when he testified in court the next day because if he told the truth they would lose. The employee said that he couldn't lie because he would be under oath. The boss replied that he could do what he liked, but "I'm just telling you: Tell the truth and you'll be fired!"

Sure enough, the employee told the truth, and his boss canned him. When he sued, the court ruled that it was the public policy of the state of California (and every other state) for people to tell the truth in court, and you couldn't fire someone for doing so. This became known as whistle-blower protection, and several different federal and state statutes, in addition to court cases, protect your employee's right to complain about legal or public policy violations in the workplace, as well as to refuse to violate the law or policy. You can't, as a manager, retaliate in any way against such people.

General Unsafe Working Conditions or Unsafe Consumer Goods

Your employees have a right to work in a safe environment. At the federal level, OSHA (the Occupational Safety and Health Administration) governs safe working environments. Many states have laws about these issues also.

Your employees have a right to complain if your company is violating OSHA standards. Moreover, if your employees complain to OSHA that you have ignored their complaints, they are protected under the whistle-blower protection described above.

The Consumer Product Safety Commission governs the safety of consumer goods. If your employees are aware that your company is making unsafe goods, they have a right to complain. If the company does not respond, the employee is protected under the whistle-blower protection laws.

To find out more about the legal issues surrounding a safe workplace, check out the Additional Resources appendix at the back of this book. For now, what's important is to be able to recognize when someone has crossed the line between being difficult and doing something illegal or otherwise violating your organization's policies or values. These situations require a very different approach from everyday workplace complaints.

Tips for Receiving Complaints

When you receive complaints about any of the legal or policy matters described above, you need to follow a very specific format in order to stay out of hot water. Consider these tips:

- Create a quiet and private place. Once you know what the complaint is, don't take it in front of a busy workplace. You should keep what the employee is telling you confidential and you should do this from the start.
- Document, document, document. As soon as you know that the employee is bringing forward one of the complaints above, start documenting. Use the documenting format discussed in Chapter 2; don't document your opinions, assumptions, or prejudices—just the verifiable facts.
- Listen and ask questions. Reserve your judgment and opinions. You should listen and ask open-ended questions, as discussed in

Chapter 3. If you can't think of another question to ask, simply keep asking "what happened next?" until the employee runs out of steam.

- Ask for details. Many employee complaints are vague (such as, "My supervisor is being unfair"). Keep asking questions in order to get the employee to be behaviorally specific: What is it that someone has specifically said or done to her to which she's objecting?

- Ask a cleanup question. At the end, be sure to ask: "Is there anything else you can tell me about this situation?" or "Is there anything else that you think I should know about this matter?"

- *Do not* issue a conclusion that the conduct was a legal or policy violation. Simply listen, ask questions, take notes, and tell the employee that you will get back to him as soon as possible.

- *Consult an expert*—legal or HR—unless you're positive that you know there's a clear violation. Even if you're sure, you need to keep HR in the loop.

- If there's any dispute about the facts, conduct an investigation. Ideally, an expert from HR or legal would be available to do this, but if not, make sure that you engage in a neutral and unbiased fact-finding.

- *If the complaint is about you, don't be defensive.* This is easier said than done, as it's human nature to be defensive, but you need to just listen and ask questions. Take a time out to calm yourself down and decide what to do next.

- Do get back to the employee. Even if all the news you have is that the investigation is ongoing about her complaint, she will appreciate your attention.

"We need to talk"

MAURICE: Susan, I'm very sorry to hear that you feel that way. Could you tell me more specifically about what you think I've done that discriminates against women? (Doesn't get defensive.)

SUSAN: Well, I just don't think we're treated the same.

MAURICE: What would be an example of that? (Asks open-ended question.)

SUSAN: The men get all the best assignments.

MAURICE: You're saying that the men get all the best assignments?

SUSAN: You gave Bob the Dean account and I received one that's much smaller. With Harry, he always gets the deals over $100,000. I never get those.

MAURICE: Well, I don't remember the details of all those assignments but I will look into it. (Documents what Susan says.) Can you think of any other examples?

SUSAN: I know that there have been others, but I can't think of them right now.

MAURICE: Well, I want you to know that I take your concerns very seriously, and I will look into the history of these assignments. In the meantime, could you review whether there have been any others and get back to me? I also want to touch base with HR, since I'm not an expert in these issues, and see what guidance they might have for us on how to handle this. (Seeks expert help.)

SUSAN: Sure.

MAURICE: Let's plan to get together in a couple of days.

Employee Conversation Don'ts	Employee Conversation Dos
Ignore law or policy.	*Educate yourself.*
Get defensive.	*Listen and ask questions.*
Fail to document.	*Document.*
Engage in this kind of behavior.	*Serve as a good role model.*
Issue an opinion about the facts.	*Listen, take notes, and call an expert.*

"We need to talk"

Chapter 9

How to Discuss Investigations, Discipline, and Suspensions

MARIA KENNEY TRIED to calm her sweaty palms and jerky movements. She needed to meet with one of her employees to tell her the results of an investigation. Susan wasn't going to like the result. It would be ugly, she knew. What she didn't know was what to do.

Investigations

It's a basic hallmark of employment law, as well as most people's values, that treatment of employees should be fair. This means doing things such as warning individuals before you terminate them, giving people feedback, and respecting their rights during discipline and suspension proceedings. It also includes doing full and fair investigations about discipline before taking action.

Investigations should be conducted if there's any doubt about the facts when you're considering discipline. Ideally, a trained HR professional or an employment lawyer would conduct the investigation, but if you're in a smaller organization, you may not have that luxury. If you end up needing to do it yourself, follow these basic principles:

- Investigations should be confidential. Only people who need to know should know. All employees you interview should be informed of this basic rule and be warned that they could be terminated or disciplined if they don't keep both the conversation you have with them, as well as the fact that they were interviewed, confidential. Inform them that they can be disciplined or terminated for violating confidentiality rules. Also, let them know that they could have individual liability for defamation—saying something false about someone that injures their reputation.

- Investigations should be neutral. What this means is that you, as the investigator, should not have any bias about what the facts or the conclusions are. You need to be unbiased.

- Ask open-ended questions. Review Chapter 3 to learn how to do this. You should not be asking any questions that suggest the answer, which might lead to allegations that you're not neutral.

- Ask for suggestions. If the investigation is being conducted because of a complaint, ask the complainant who else they think should be interviewed or what other evidence they're aware of that should be considered. Ask the accused and witnesses the same thing.

- Listen well. You should be doing 20 percent or less of the talking and listening 80 percent of the time. If that ratio is reversed, it's not an investigation, it's a lecture.

- Document well. Use the documentation tips from Chapter 2, but basically, just document verifiable facts, not your conclusions, your assumptions, or your biases.

- Check e-mail. Be sure to check the e-mails of the people involved for the relevant periods. Many times in recent years, an entire investigation has turned on what was said in an e-mail. People seem to think that e-mail is a place for their own private thoughts. It's not. The "e" in e-mail could just as easily stand for "evidence." Your company owns the e-mail system and the computer, and if employees are sending and receiving e-mail through your network and equipment, you have every right to check it.

- Confer with the experts. Try to find an HR consultant or employment law attorney with whom to review your results before you take action.
- Allow people to vent. Investigations are emotionally charged situations, creating a wave of upsets through any work group. You would do well to allow whomever you're interviewing to spill all his emotions and feelings while you listen. Many times, employees need to rid themselves of the emotions surrounding the situation before they can truly focus on the facts.

How to Manage Your Emotions and Theirs During Disciplining or Investigations

Conducting investigations or disciplining employees may bring about some of the most emotionally charged conversations you'll ever have with employees. In order to survive the ordeal, you must manage your emotions and theirs.

Most of us respond to conflict situations such as these in automatic, emotional ways. Those of us who tend toward the more aggressive style of conflict management go into an automatic fight mode. Those who avoid conflict tend to go into flight mode.

One explanation for this is the very structure of the brain. Physical anthropologists who study the development of the brain call the most basic parts of the human brain the reptilian brain, and tell us that old part of our brain resembles the brains of a reptile. When reptiles are stressed, they automatically respond with an instinct for flight or fight. When our back is against the wall, humans retain this instinct as well.

To understand how this might work, imagine an avocado. The fleshy part of the avocado is the largest part of the brain, the emotional part. The skin of the avocado serves as the thinking part of the brain, a kind of manual override. The pit represents the unconscious part of the brain—basically, we have no idea what's going on there. Our task is to try to develop and access the thinking part of our brain, to override the emotional part and react with thoughts—not just our instinctive emotions—during conflict.

We need to step back during stress and conflict and understand the difference between our own emotional reactions and thinking reactions. When we react emotionally during conflict, we're frequently generating and sustaining *personality* conflicts instead of productive conflicts over ideas, theories, and programs.

If you look at your own style and habitual response to stressful situations, such as disciplining an employee, you'll be able to see where you fall on the spectrum of approaching or avoiding conflict. Neither extreme will serve you when you're trying to help an employee improve, which is the purpose of feedback and discipline. Aggressive styles simply steamroll over others' needs and interests. Conflict avoiders also do not understand the creative potential in conflict.

Most managers primarily use one style in conflict situations. They use this style when considering new ideas and problems of conflict within themselves as well as when they interact with others. What you need to do is notice the style you're using and pick the right style for the right situation.

For example, because of my training as an attorney, I tend to use an analytical, argumentative, and critical conflict resolution style. When I'm handling employee feedback or discipline matters, I have to force myself to step back and use a different style. If I don't guard against this tendency, I will, without thinking, begin to debate instead of discuss when the employee wants to vent her own feelings or raise a new issue.

Although debating may be a useful skill when engaged in an actual debate, courtroom battle, or a dispute with the plumber, this style creates disadvantages in personal and most professional relationships. Debate is not conducive to seeing the creative spark in conflict. Rather, the debater is often running over the needs and feelings of others.

This style may make the employee confrontation seem easy, but it often causes the people on the receiving end to shut down or tuck their heads in order to avoid having them torn off. It doesn't allow them to express their emotions, foster creative solutions, or help them learn how to solve their own problems.

Negative Criticism and Confrontation

When you're conducting an investigation, delivering bad news, or disciplining an employee, consider trying to do it in the most productive way possible. You're taking these steps to improve the workplace environment and help individual employees improve.

Be sure not to use negative criticism for revenge when an employee has done something wrong or to hurt someone by doing a poor job. For example, if you were to say, "Jill, your report was bad. How could you do such terrible work?", that would be unhelpful feedback. This criticism doesn't help the coworker learn because it neither specifically describes what Jill did wrong, identifies what behavior would be acceptable, creatively manages the conflict, or helps her improve. This type of criticism leaves the recipient feeling demoralized and doesn't foster learning or correction. Ask yourself why you would offer such a critique. If you're not allowing someone to change his behavior or skills so the work can improve, why are you saying it?

A better way to deliver this feedback would be to say, "Jill, I noticed that when you typed this report you didn't use the margins I specified. We need to stay within a certain page count to fit the form. Also, when you answered the phone just now, you didn't ask how you could help the caller. Please do that in the future."

This criticism improves the learner because it lets Jill know what she did and when, and how the other party was affected.

Here's a list of techniques that contribute to unskillful confrontation:

- Failing to address the point and instead, talking around the issue
- Confronting someone while angry, which can lead to you lashing out and damage the relationship
- Giving feedback only at yearly performance reviews or when an employee needs discipline
- Discussing an issue with a third party rather than the employee directly involved
- Being vague and not giving examples of specific practices where the employee can improve

Curiosity or Confrontation

When you feel the need to confront an employee about an issue and impose discipline, consider changing your own attitude before you talk to her. Can you find a way to be *curious* about the other person's behavior? If you come from a place of curiosity and wonder, the interaction will have a much better chance of succeeding. Consider *reframing* your confrontation to use the following statements:

- I'm *puzzled* by your behavior. Can you explain to me how it would help our team meet our goals?
- I was *curious* about why you did X. Can you explain your behavior to me?
- I'm *confused* by the statement you made yesterday about X. Can you explain to me how you believe it will help us finish this job?

There are, of course, some personality types who value direct confrontations, including the pit-bulls among us. These employees may want you to tell them straight away what the problem is and how you want them to do it differently. This "curiosity" technique works best when there's a big power differential between the speaker and the listener, or when you know that you have a tendency to come on too strong and that people will not be able to hear what you say when you're that abrupt.

More Land Mines to Avoid

Be prepared for defensiveness. Most employees feel defensive when you're disciplining them or reporting the results of an investigation that did not go the way they had hoped. Most of us feel defensive when we're receiving feedback or criticism, even when it's skillfully delivered. If we're speeding and the state patrol stops us, for example, most of us do not jump out of our car and declare: "Oh, thank you officer! I'm so glad you stopped me! I could have hurt someone! Write me a ticket immediately!"

When you notice that your negative feedback frequently leads to defensiveness, another reason may be that you offer complaints without requests. As the popular psychologist Gay Hendricks points out in his book *Conscious Living*:

*　　*　　*

"If every ounce of energy human beings use in complaining was dedicated to productive change, we could clear up many of the world's problems virtually overnight. It takes courage to turn a complaint into a request for effective action. It requires that you think about what needs to be done rather than about what wasn't done. It requires that you get outside the negative-thinking cycle of 'What's wrong with me? What's wrong with you? What's wrong with the world?' and make a courageous leap of thought to 'Forget what's wrong—let's focus on what needs to be done.'"

*　　*　　*

If you're generating a "flight or fight" mode in an employee during investigations or discipline, you may want to step back and examine whether you're expressing your emotions in the most skillful ways. If you rage at someone, or alternatively, if you're holding in your emotions and have a stony expression, you may trigger a flight-or-fight response in another. Most of us have not really thought about or practiced the appropriate expression of emotion, especially during feedback and conflict. What is the most effective way to *express* strong feelings without *dumping* them on someone?

Using Emotions for Successful Confrontations

The best way to communicate your own emotions while you're giving someone feedback or discipline is in a straightforward way. Think of it as a weather report: "It's raining and I'm angry." Your feelings change just as the weather does, and you can report on what you experience without blaming or judging an employee for causing your emotions. When you do this, the other person is better able to hear what we're saying. We don't need to dramatize or hide the weather; like our feelings, it just is what it is.

While describing the effect someone's behavior has on your workgroup can be helpful, people are more likely to be able to hear you if you use "I" statements and stay neutral in your report. For example, people may be more receptive to hear you say "I'm angry," instead of "You make me angry."

When we decide it's necessary, we can, before we state the problem or discipline and communicate our request, add a clear expression of feelings. Consider the following examples:

✻　✻　✻

Jill, *I'm angry.* I just realized that you didn't finish the report on time. When our reports are late, it puts the entire production schedule behind our goals. From now on, I need you to turn them in on time or let me know well in advance that you can't do it so I can find someone else.

Harry, my stomach feels queasy and I just realized that *I'm afraid.* When you yell at your team, I'm afraid you're going to hit someone. I need you to stop yelling and give them directions in a normal tone of voice.

✻　✻　✻

Expressing your emotions this clearly and without drama during a confrontation takes practice. Many of us have not thought about the idea of this kind of emotional practice. Have you ever received good modeling or suggestions from your parents or taken a class on appropriate emotional expression? Cleanly offered emotion can make our feedback to others clearer and more congruent. If you deliver bad news with a forced smile because you're struggling to contain your anger, for example, you trigger uncertainty about your message or worse in the other person. Employees have built-in radar that can be highly attuned to the emotions of others. Conversely, if you're out of control with your anger, or if you yell and use profanity when you offer feedback, the employee may freeze, flee, or fight back. When you don't offer your own feelings in an appropriate way, something frequently feels scary, false, or confusing to the other party and makes your feedback less effective than it could be.

Sometimes, the problem is that managers become defensive themselves when they're offering feedback to someone. When this happens, you may want to examine whether you're speaking to try to help the employee learn and grow, or speaking from your own defensiveness.

For instance, when you're talking to someone you might notice that he starts frowning and looking away. Because you're *sure* that you're correct in your assessment of him, you may be tempted to say: "I don't know why what I'm saying makes you angry; you're the one who messed up this project." In putting it this way, you've just revealed your own defensiveness, which will probably prompt them to respond in kind.

Instead, if you notice someone frowning and avoiding your gaze while you are giving feedback, you can offer something like: "I just noticed an expression on your face. I'm wondering what you're feeling about what I just said?" Although it might feel awkward to use this discovery method at first, you can become more skilled at the practice. Eventually, using this method of communicating will reduce the amount of defensiveness you trigger in others during feedback and discipline.

Be Aware of Past Issues with Conflict

Another land mine to avoid is triggering memories in someone of past criticism. Many times an employee will explode over what you might think of as relatively minor feedback or discipline. Most employees have received plenty of negative and unhelpful feedback from parents and teachers as children, and workplace criticism tends to remind us of those past wounds. If an employee reacts out of proportion to the event, this may be part of the reason.

Stick to the issue and try not to react yourself. If you don't control your own emotions, the problem may never be managed creatively. Take a time out if you find yourself losing control. Be sure, however, not to give up. You may need to schedule additional sessions before the conflict moves to a higher level.

Additional Investigation Issues

When an employee makes a complaint about a legal or policy violation, you're obligated to do an investigation. You have an obligation to learn all the facts, especially the accused person's side of the story. You should do everything you can to be fair during the course of the investigation. Anything you say or do that appears to be less than neutral or that indicates bias or prejudice can be used against you later.

"We need to talk"

You may need to go back and talk more than once with witnesses or anyone who has relevant information. Investigations can be a complex tangle of the facts and circumstances, and it's helpful to not only keep good notes but to chart out what you need.

Workplace Versus Criminal Investigations

The rules in workplace investigations are different from investigations conducted by the police, and employees have different rights in each situation. Many times people assume that what they've seen on *Law & Order* governs workplace investigations and start asserting that they have a right to an attorney, a right to confront their accuser, or other claims.

Not true. While employers are obligated to conduct internal investigations in these situations, different rules apply for workplace investigations than for criminal investigations. If the misconduct could involve a crime, there may also be a parallel police investigation going on and, in that situation, the rules of criminal investigations would apply to the problem. But with workplace investigations, the standard is that an employer conduct a "full and fair investigation and come to a reasonable conclusion."

You may even come to the wrong conclusion, but as long as your conclusion is reasonable, you carried out a good investigation. An important Oregon Supreme Court opinion exemplifies this standard. In that case, two women allegedly made violent threats against a coworker. The employer conducted an investigation; they questioned witnesses. The accused employees were informed of the charges against them and the employees gave their side of the story. They denied making threats. After listening to everyone, the company believed the accusing employees and fired the two women.

The women sued for wrongful termination. They said they didn't make threats and that they could prove that they didn't, but the court at that point found their proof irrelevant.

The court said that even if the investigation turned up the wrong result, the company still couldn't be sued for wrongful termination. As long as the company conducted a sufficient investigation, it acted fairly. The possibility that they might have come to the wrong conclusion was irrelevant.

This standard is in contrast to criminal investigation and trials where you must be found guilty "beyond a reasonable doubt." This is a very high standard, unlike civil disputes, such as employment lawsuits, where the standard is "a preponderance of the evidence." What that means is if there's some evidence on each side, you go with the side with the most evidence, even if it's just a featherweight more.

During the investigation, everyone has a right to be treated with respect, even the accused. You can question but not interrogate. What's the difference? If you're asking open-ended questions and listening respectfully, it's questioning. If you're accusing or bullying the person you're questioning, it's an interrogation. You do have a right to ask questions and your employer's policies (reflected in employee handbooks or other documents) may contain words requiring employees to cooperate with any internal investigations. Employees can be disciplined or terminated for failing to follow these internal rules.

Although employees don't have a right to have an attorney present at work, they do have a right to contact an attorney on their own time. They may also have a right, under a union contract, to have a union representative present. They have a right to know what specific behavior they're accused of engaging in, as well as the exact policy or law they've violated. They do not have a right to know who accused them of this behavior, nor is there any Fifth Amendment right to confront their accuser. The Fifth Amendment only applies to criminal investigations.

If an employee believes that she was terminated without a full and fair investigation, that she was the subject of an investigation because of discrimination, or that you didn't come to a reasonable conclusion, she may have a right to sue for wrongful termination and/or discrimination.

The employee has a right to have what he says—as well as the entire investigation—kept confidential. Only those who need to know should be aware that there's even an investigation going on. If there's a lot of gossip about the investigation going around the workplace, you can and should put a stop to it. If the statements made about an employee to people who are not involved in the investigation are false and damaging to his or her reputation, the defamed may have a claim for defamation.

Everyone involved, but especially managers and the accused, needs to be warned not to retaliate against the complainant.

Making a Determination

Once you've completed a fair and thorough investigation, you need to decide whether the complaint or accusation has merit. This is where many investigators wimp out and start fussing about not having enough "proof." Often, they're stuck on thinking that they have to prove the claim "beyond a reasonable doubt." When they refocus their thoughts on "a preponderance of the evidence," they may indeed be able to decide what they think.

If you have a statement from the complainant, that is evidence—if you believe him or her.

Many workplace investigations boil down to a swearing contest between two employees. Managers serving as investigators don't like to decide who is telling the truth. Yet, courts and juries decide swearing contests every day, so it's a good idea to make that judgment call. If you don't, someone else will down the road.

Especially in delicate situations such as harassment investigations, many managers fear that someone could file a false complaint and ruin someone else's career. Totally false complaints in this area are rare. Just because it's one person's word against another's doesn't mean that the case is false.

What is common is for two people to be involved in the same situation and come away from it with totally different perspectives about what happened. Neither one of them is lying; they're just both really wedded to their own perspective.

You should examine credibility. Look at whether either the accused or the complainant has a reason to lie.

> **"We need to talk"**
>
> Sometimes investigators believe that the employee who is complaining acted irrationally. That also happened in the Clarence Thomas–Anita Hill situation. Many senators said they didn't believe Professor Hill because she acted irrationally, following him to another job after he harassed her at the EEOC. Even after she left that job, she saw him twice and talked with him on the phone. She also recommended to the FBI that he be appointed to the Court.

It's common for victims of harassment, discrimination, threats, or violence in the workplace to act irrationally. They've been traumatized and frequently don't know where to turn or how to act.

Other options may not appear to them. They may have allowed the behavior to go on for a long time, because we've all been taught— especially women—to try to get along. That doesn't mean the alleged behavior didn't happen.

Take Corrective Action—Discipline or Suspension

If you find the behavior occurred, you must take what's called "corrective action." That can include discipline, suspension, or termination.

In the case of harassment and discrimination, whatever action you take must be sufficient to make the behavior stop. If you take action and the behavior doesn't stop, what you did wasn't sufficient.

When you're administering any discipline, you should make certain that you're fair and consistent. What that means is that you should consider what discipline has been implemented in similar situations. You'll need to ask HR or other managers if you don't have a baseline for such situations in your organization. Follow all your policies and procedures about discipline. The person who makes decisions regarding employment matters is the one who needs to be consistent. Sometimes this can be a tricky thing to figure out.

For example, at the remote operating station for an electrical utility company, there were two sides to the operating station. Each side was operated by a separate manager with a director over both sides.

One side of the station was managed by a new manager who was a "by-the-book" manager. He opened up the employee manual and did whatever it said for that particular situation. The other manager had worked for the company for twenty years and worked his way up from being on the line with the other men. He had known most of the men for years, and drank and bowled with them.

The by-the-book manager had a workforce that had always been primarily Latino. A man on that side got into a fight in the parking lot. The new manager checked the policies, saw that they had a strict policy on threats and violence, and gave him thirty days suspension without pay.

The other side of the operating station was primarily Caucasian. On that side, a man also got into a fight in the parking lot and the older manager there said, "Oh that's just Scotty. He doesn't mean anything." He gave him two days suspension with pay to "think about his behavior."

The Latino gentleman heard about the difference and complained to the EEOC. The EEOC found that they had been inconsistent because the decision maker, the director of the operating station, ultimately had the authority to make discipline decisions, even though he followed the recommendations of the other two managers. The lesson here is that you need to make sure that you've thought about who the decision maker might be, and that person needs to be consistent.

Discipline needs to be progressive if you have a progressive discipline policy or if you have a union or other contract that requires it.

Discipline can include any of the following:

- Verbal warning
- Written warning
- Paid suspension
- Unpaid suspension
- Termination

Follow-up

After you've resolved an investigation or delivered some kind of discipline, you should follow up to make sure that what you did was effective. You should also follow up after an investigation to let the complainant and the accused know the results of your finding. The complainant doesn't have a right to know what discipline was entered, but you can just say: "We did a full and complete investigation and found that your complaint did (or did not) have merit. We have taken appropriate corrective action." Some companies do tell the victim exactly what corrective action has been taken, and asked him to keep it confidential. The courts have allowed this.

If you do find that someone has been victimized, you need to follow up with her at two weeks, at four weeks, and at six weeks. After that point, you can just direct her to let you know if she has any more problems.

If you do not find merit to the complaint, and the complainant is unhappy with the result, you can give him a sanitized summary of the investigation, that is, the bare-bones details of the investigation. You could say, "We interviewed six witnesses, everyone you suggested, and looked at all the relevant e-mails," or something similar.

You should also go back to the witnesses and tell them that the investigation has been completed and thank them for their cooperation. Remind them that their participation in the investigation must be kept confidential.

A Final Note on Confidentiality

Everything about investigations, discipline, warnings, and the related documentation should be kept in the strictest confidence. Ideally, these kinds of investigation reports, warnings, and disciplinary memos should be kept in a locked file in HR or in your office if you don't have an HR department. Don't talk with other managers about this if they're not involved in the situation. You should contact security if you believe that the employee may act out violently.

Sample Script — *"We need to talk"*

MARIA: Susan, we need to let you know about the results of our investigation.

SUSAN: Yes?

MARIA: We found no merit to your complaint. (Get straight to the point.)

SUSAN: I can't believe that!

MARIA: I understand. I want you to know that we take these matters very seriously and that we did a very thorough investigation. We interviewed ten witnesses in all, including everyone you suggested. We also looked at all the relevant e-mail. (Offers a sanitized summary of the investigation.) I understand how you could have perceived the events differently, but we don't think that the behavior was intentional, nor did it rise to the level of a legal or policy violation. Is there anyone else that you think we should have interviewed other than the people we already talked about?

SUSAN: Not that I can think of. I'm really disappointed in this result.

MARIA: I understand. What we are going to do is bring in a facilitator to work with the entire group in order for you all to work better together. I think that will help with some of your concerns. I want you to know that we appreciate you coming forward. Please let me know if anything else comes up.

Employee Conversation Don'ts	Employee Conversation Dos
Beat around the bush.	Get straight to the point.
Engage in cross-examination.	Ask open-ended questions.
Treat people differently.	Be consistent.
Talk too much.	Keep things confidential.
Finish the investigation without letting the complainant know the result.	Follow up.
Skip discipline steps without a compelling reason.	Follow progressive discipline policies.

Chapter 10

How to Word Terminations, Layoffs, or Responses to People Leaving

SAM BROWN WALKED down the hall to Chandra's office wishing that he could fly out the nearest window. He needed to fire her. He'd never terminated anyone before. He had absolutely, positively no idea what to say.

Terminations

As mentioned elsewhere in this book, terminations are one area of the law where the courts have required fairness. This means that before termination, employees have been warned, counseled, and told to improve so that there are no surprises.

You may have heard the term *at-will employee*. Most states are "at-will" states, which means that theoretically, you can fire anyone at any time for any reason. However, the "at-will" doctrine has been eroded so much with exceptions that you have to assume one of the exceptions applies before you terminate someone. The main exceptions are that you can't terminate (or take any other "wrongful action" such as failing to promote or failing to give other perks) if to do so would

- Violate public policy (meaning that you have to protect whistle-blowers);
- Violate a contract. Contracts can be informal, such as an employee manual or things you verbally promised an employee; or
- Violate the "covenant of good faith and fair dealing." This basically means that you have to be fair—warn before firing, give employees honest feedback, and so on.

Assuming that one of these exceptions does not apply, you can go ahead and terminate someone.

As mentioned in the last chapter, you have to be consistent when it comes to disciplining and terminating employees. You have to give the same discipline for the same type of misconduct. You can't fire one employee for poor performance if another employee with similar poor performance isn't fired. You should follow your progressive discipline policy if you have one.

> **"We need to talk"**
>
> If you've allowed employees to break the rules, or even encouraged rule breaking, the courts have found it unfair if you then turn around and fire them.

Be careful that you're only terminating them for something that's business-related. In most situations, you should not be firing employees for something that they said or did away from work, unless their conduct bleeds back into the workplace and affects their coworkers.

Be Straightforward about Termination

If you've followed all the steps for giving people accurate information about their performance, giving accurate performance reviews, warned them, and completed a thorough investigation, if necessary, the actual termination should be obvious. You should say something really simple, such as "You were told to improve but you didn't so you're being terminated today."

Of course, if someone is being fired for misconduct, you can fire them immediately after you make a good factual determination. It wouldn't be reasonable to have to wait.

Many managers do not tell the truth about firing. Sometimes they want to sugarcoat the truth by telling employees that there's been reorganization or that their job was eliminated. Don't go down that slippery slope. If you tell them one of these stories, and they find out the truth, they're more likely to think that you were lying to them about other things and more likely to go straight to an attorney. Courts find this to be unfair as well. This is especially true if you have a progressive discipline policy as a part of your employee handbook or other contract. If so, you have to follow it and not fabricate a reorganization or job elimination.

What Else to Do

As you gain more experience as a manager, you may realize that it's not the employees that you fire who drive you crazy—it's the ones you don't fire.

If you've followed progressive discipline, it should be no surprise to the employee when you say you're being terminated. There are a number of other steps you might consider in order to look fair and humane.

Decide if the employee can stay for a time—perhaps a few weeks—as a transition while they look for another job. Sometimes you can't do this or it would be a problem for other employees.

Also, always let security know that you're doing a termination. They don't need to be in the office with you—unless you think there's a potential for danger—but let them stand by just in case. If you don't have security, make sure that some other manager is nearby or in the office. Unfortunately, many incidents of violence in the workplace occur after terminations.

Once you decide to tell the employee she's being terminated, get straight to the point and end the pain quickly. Be sure to do the termination in private in a conference room or her office so you can walk away if you need to.

If you do give the employee some transition time, do an exit interview on their last day. You may learn something useful. Even if you don't, it allows an employee an opportunity to express all her feelings. If they do this, she may be less likely to think that she needs to sue or pursue some other way of getting even.

"We need to talk"

Many managers fire employees on a Friday, which is a mistake. This gives them all weekend to stew with nothing to do until Monday. Instead, you should fire them when they reach the end of their warning period.

The reasons behind the termination should be confidential. In one case, a manager told all the other employees that a twenty-year veteran of the company had been fired for being dishonest. He sued for defamation and won $200,000. The company wasn't able to prove he'd been dishonest at trial, even though the court held that they had a legitimate reason to fire him because they'd done a sufficient investigation.

Never fire an employee in front of other people, or when you're emotional or exploding. If necessary, you can suspend the employee while you do an investigation and consider your options. Cool off, and then if you decide to fire, you can convert the suspension into a termination.

In order to be perceived as fair, you should also do the following:

- Consider allowing employees to use the office to make phone calls, and use e-mail while they look for another job.
- Avoid discussing them with other potential employees so you look fair and avoid defamation charges.
- Pay all of their commissions and paychecks, including accrued vacation.
- Provide severance while they're unemployed.
- Don't contest their applications for unemployment benefits.
- Offer outplacement services.

All these suggestions are expensive, but they're cheaper than a lawsuit. They also build goodwill among your employees and potential employees.

Layoffs

Of course, businesses can have layoffs or RIF (reductions in force). In some states and companies, a layoff means that you have to offer the employees who were laid off their jobs back if they become open again. A RIF refers to a permanent reduction.

Obviously, you should follow all your company's procedures and policies in doing the layoff. Courts will generally not question whether there was a business reason for the layoff. Some traps, however, include situations in which the layoff isn't really a layoff but an attempt to get rid of older or more expensive workers. Even if you don't believe this is the intent, you need to look at the numbers to make sure that there's not what the courts call a "disproportionate impact" on the oldest workers or any other group with a particular protected characteristic.

The courts will question things if you don't consistently apply the criteria for the layoff or if the layoff isn't legitimate. If the laid-off employee is replaced within six months, the RIF looks suspicious. Even if you give the new employee a different job title, it looks phony.

If you have a layoff and then your budget is restored, you should call the people you laid off and give them an opportunity to come back to work. Even if you've restructured the job, you should interview the laid-off employees as a matter of fairness; they may be able to do the new job.

If you're using a legitimate layoff to get rid of a nonperformer, you should have documentation to back up the nonperformance.

You should have legitimate criteria for the layoff. The criteria should be in writing, and it should be company- or department-wide. Allowing one manager to decide about his or her own criteria is dangerous.

Under the WARN Act, a company with 100 or more employees must give sixty days of notice for certain types of layoffs or plant closings. If you don't follow this rule, you must pay employees one day's pay for every day less than sixty days.

When you talk with your employees about layoffs, again, it should be very simple. Tell them the truth, whatever the legitimate business reason might be. If you can offer severance packages and outplacement counseling, it will serve you well in the long run. Employees are less likely to sue if they've received these benefits.

Last but not least, express compassion. It's a big deal for most employees to lose their job. Tell them how sorry you are, and let them express whatever emotions they have. Studies consistently show that employees who are treated with dignity and respect tend to sue less often than other employees. Even when you're delivering the bad news you can act humanely.

What to Say When Someone Quits

When a valued employee quits, many managers just throw up their hands and seem to assume a "what can I do" attitude. This doesn't serve you and it may not serve the employee.

Employees quit for many reasons. They may have legitimately found a better job, they may be suffering from bullying or harassment (unknown to you) in your department, or they may be bored or feeling unchallenged. What's important for you to consider is that their announcement may just be one more opportunity to open a dialogue rather than a sign that you should simply surrender and agree that they're leaving you.

If the employee is someone you want to retain, you should fight and fight hard to get her to stay. Replacing employees is expensive, anywhere from 100 to 150 percent of the employee's salary. It's well worth the investment of your time and energy to see if you can change her mind. Ask her these questions in order to start a dialogue:

- What was going on in your workgroup when you first thought about leaving? (Employees almost always say that they're leaving because they received a better job offer, more money, or a better opportunity. If you ask what was going on when they first started thinking about leaving, however, you may find a very different reason for the departure.)
- What did you like best about your job?
- What did you like least about your job?
- What's the one thing that would change your mind about leaving?
- Would you be willing to talk to our director (or president, or CEO, depending upon the company) and see what input he might have on your decision?

Usually, this series of questions will help clarify what's really going on with the employee and what, if anything, you can do about her decision. Try to create a dialogue during this discussion. Don't cut her off or argue with her, but keep asking open-ended questions to gain as much information as possible.

> **"We need to talk"**
>
> Listen hard. You may hear information that you hadn't heard before that would lead you to a new conclusion about what might help keep this particular employee around.

Don't get angry. Don't burn bridges with the employee. You never know when he may come back. McKinsey, a successful consulting company, is so accustomed to people leaving and coming back to the firm that they actually have clubs and newsletters for McKinsey alumni, what they call "boomerangs." Let the employee know that the door is always open.

If the employee is someone that you were not sorry to lose, simply wish her well and leave it at that.

Sample Script

"We need to talk"

SAM: (Walking into Chandra's office so that he can leave when he needs to.) Chandra, I need to talk to you privately. (He closes the door.)

CHANDRA: Okay.

SAM: You know we've had a number of conversations about your performance over the last year. Unfortunately, it hasn't improved, so we're going to have to terminate you. (Gets right to the point.)

CHANDRA: Well, I thought I was making progress.

SAM: I'm afraid not. And if you look at the follow-up meeting notes that we took after your last performance review, I warned you that we would have to terminate you if these things didn't improve. We are going to give you the use of your office for the next three weeks so that you can start searching for a new job, and we are offering you outplacement counseling. HR will also be talking with you about a severance package. (Offers an office, outplacement, and severance.)

CHANDRA: Well, I do appreciate that.

SAM: I'm sorry things didn't work out.

Employee Conversation Don'ts	Employee Conversation Dos
Drag things out.	*Get right to the point.*
Give up when someone quits.	*Fight for a good employee.*
Make your own rules for layoffs.	*Follow the written policies.*

"We need to talk"

Chapter 11

How to Know What Your Employees Are Thinking Before You Talk with Them

GRETA RILEY LOOKED over the shop floor and shook her head. All thirty of her employees looked busy, but something told her that some of them lacked the energy and engagement she needed to create real success with her business. Many of her employees were new twenty-something employees. Greta was their first boss. She'd tried all the standard management tools: giving pep talks providing feedback, trying rewards programs, but something was still lacking. What she really needed, she decided, was a mind reader. Unfortunately, she had no idea how to know what her employees were thinking.

Mind reading might seem to be an odd skill in a book about conversations, but sometimes you can talk and talk and listen and listen and still feel as if you're not getting to the bottom of whatever is going on with your employees. Here's what your employees would say if you could read their minds:

- Pay attention to me!
- Give me criticism in small bites.
- Don't stonewall or sulk if I've done something wrong.
- Help me discover my strengths and weaknesses.
- Give me the amount of supervision I need.
- During change, let me know what resources I'll have to cope.

How to Listen So That Your Employees Will Talk

First, try this technique. Set aside fifteen minutes every week to meet with each of your direct reports. During those meetings, ask two questions:

1. Is there anything that I'm doing or that anyone else is doing here that's interfering with your success?
2. Is there anything that I could do or that anyone else could do that would make you more successful?

When you first start having these regular meetings, what kind of a response do you think you'll receive? That's right, they'll probably say nothing. If you keep asking week after week, they'll eventually start opening up. At that point, of course, your task is to listen and listen hard.

Frequently, managers think that they've been asking open-ended questions and listening to their employees, but most of them have not really learned how to listen well. That's because it's hard: Most people never learn how.

Part of the problem is that we live in an increasingly visual world with screens everywhere: computers, video games, TV, and movies. We don't sit around the kitchen table telling stories often enough. We move fast. Listening requires that we slow down.

You can, however, become passionate in your listening. Instead of listening for evidence that confirms your point of view, you can listen with the creative energy and enthusiasm that you put into talking. Listen for the creative energy in the conflict—both in yourselves and in others—and for challenges to your own point of view in order to understand how others see the world.

When you do decide to listen, try to find out what the other person's "good enough reason" is. What you'll discover is that people do not behave as irrationally as you might think. People do what they do for good-enough reasons. They may not seem like good reasons to you or me, but they're good-enough reasons for them. If your employees understand that you're sincerely trying to find out what motivates *them*, they will open up and tell you the most surprising things.

When you do decide to listen to find out what the employee's "good-enough reason" might be, follow these tips:

1. Remember filters. We all hear what is said through our own filters. Filters can include our assumptions, biases, history, experience, and so forth.

2. Listen as a witness. Ask, "How would I listen to this person if I knew I was going to be called as an objective witness in court?" "How can I listen well enough to hear the still, small voice inside me that tells me what they're saying is true?"

3. Clarify. Before you speak, make sure you understand what the other person is saying. Ask open-ended, nonleading questions (who, what, where, when) until you do understand.

4. Restate. Ask, "I think you said 'X', is that accurate?" Continue restating until your employee agrees that you heard him or her accurately.

5. Pause before you speak. Ask yourself if the style you're using will serve you best over the long term. Is the response you're considering likely to lead to more satisfaction for you, and more creativity and productivity for your team? What response would be most likely to lead to those results?

6. At the end of a communication, summarize the conversation and clarify the original reason for the communication. Did the speaker want your advice, feedback, a sympathetic ear, action, or a solution to a problem? Be sure you know why you were asked to listen and what you're expected to do—if anything—about the communication. Many managers jump in too quickly to give advice or fix a problem before even bothering to ask if the speaker wants advice.

7. Assume 100 percent of the responsibility for the communication. Assume leadership in your communication with employees. Assume that it is your responsibility to listen until you understand and to speak in a way others can understand.

8. Check out misunderstandings. Assume miscommunication before you assume that someone is trying to undermine your efforts. Effective communication is the exception, not the rule.

Sample Script

"We need to talk"

GRETA: Sammy, I just wanted to check in with you today to see how you're doing. As you know, I like to have weekly check-ins with my staff.

SAMMY: Yes, I know.

GRETA: Well, as you also know, I like to follow a specific format for these meetings, asking you whether there's anything that I'm doing or that anyone else here is doing that's interfering with your success and also if there's anything that I could do that would help you be more successful. (Persists in asking these questions, even if she's had no luck in the past.) Any thoughts today?

SAMMY: Well, I do like my job but sometimes things do get a little slow back in my department, and I like to be busy. I've been looking at the new computer system and I have ideas about how it might work better. I wasn't sure if it was my place to bring it up, though.

GRETA: Well, you know, I've been tearing my hair out over that system. I'd love to hear your thoughts. I didn't realize that you had an interest in that area. Tell me more.

SAMMY: Well, I don't have any formal IT training. It's just something that I've always liked and been good at.

GRETA: I'm glad to know that. Let's plan some time to get together and talk about what you think and what you'd like to do. Maybe we can come up with some additional training opportunities also.

SAMMY: Thanks. I'd like that.

Employee Conversation Don'ts	Employee Conversation Dos
Fail to listen.	*Listen with passion.*
Ignore employees.	*Get to know them.*
Give them complex feedback.	*Give them brief, direct feedback.*
Focus only on what you need.	*Help them develop strengths and weaknesses.*

"We need to talk"

Conclusion

While conversations with your employees may seem complicated, it boils down to a few simple rules:

- Be fair. If what you're saying or doing doesn't seem fair to you, it's unlikely to seem that way to your employees, a court, or a jury.
- Give employees honest feedback and listen to theirs.
- Document, document, document. Keep track of your employee conversations and have employees e-mail them back to you so that you know your words were understood.
- Be consistent. Be careful not to say one thing to one employee and give another a totally different set of rules or feedback.
- Seek expert help. If at all possible, it's always a good idea to check with HR or legal advisors whenever you're unsure.
- Manage your emotions. Employees can push your buttons in ways that can make it challenging to be calm. Try to vent with someone else, or write down your feelings before you have a difficult employee conversation. This preparation will pay off for you in the long run.
- Use this book as a tool. Before you have a difficult conversation, review the Dos and Don'ts at the end of that relevant chapter.

Managing people can seem intimidating and a chore, but if you follow these few simple rules, you can turn it into a pleasure. Managing people is simply another chance to create a relationship with someone. Focus on connection. That's what gives any relationship energy and makes it worth your while to manage. If you do that, you'll find that the road ahead smoothes out, and you will gain confidence in your management abilities. Studying the suggestions in this book will pay off in terms of the investment of your time and energy. I wish you continued success on your journey.

"We need to talk"

Appendix A

Additional Resources

9 to 5, National Association of Working Women
www.members.aol.com/naww925

American Civil Liberties Union
www.aclu.org

American Federation of Labor-Congress of Industrial Organizations (AFL-CIO)
www.aflcio.org

Asian American Legal Defense and Educational Fund (AALDEF)
E-mail: *AALDEF@worldnet.att.net*

Equal Employment Opportunity Commission (EEOC)
www.eeoc.gov

Mexican American Legal Defense and Educational Fund (MALDEF)
www.maldef.org

NAACP Legal Defense and Education Fund, Inc.
www.naacp.org

National Employment Lawyers Association (NELA)
www.nela.org

National Organization for Women (NOW)
www.now.org

Legal Defense and Education Fund
www.nowldef.org

www.salary.com

www.workingamerica.org/badboss

Appendix B

Bibliography

Eisaguirre, Lynne. *The Power of a Good Fight*. Indianapolis: Literary Architects. 2006.

Goleman, Daniel. *Social Intelligence: The New Science of Relationships*. New York: Bantam, Reprint Edition, 1997.

Hallowell, Edward M. *Connect*. New York: Pantheon, 1999.

Hendricks, Gay. *Conscious Living: Finding Joy in the Real World*. San Francisco: HarperOne, 2001.

Shenk, David. *Data Smog: Surviving the Glut*. San Francisco: HarperOne, Rev. Upd. Ed. 1998.

Sutherland, Amy. *Kicked, Bitten and Scratched: Life Lessons at the World's Premier School for Exotic Animal Trainers*. New York: Viking, 2006.

Index